G R A P H I S   L E T T E R H E A D   2

GRAPHIS LETTERHEAD 2

The International Survey of Letterhead Design

Ein internationaler Überblick über die Gestaltung von Briefpapier

Une Vue d'Ensemble de la Création Internationale de Papiers a Lettres

Edited by · Herausgegeben von · Edité par:

B. Martin Pedersen

Publisher and Creative Director: B. Martin Pedersen

Editors: Annette Crandall, Heinke Jenssen

Associate Editor: Kimberly E. Morris

Art Directors: B. Martin Pedersen, Randell Pearson

Graphis Press Corp. Zürich (Switzerland)

(OPPOSITE PAGE)
Client: OHIO STATE UNIVERSITY Design Firm: RICKABAUGH GRAPHICS
Art Directors: ERIC RICKABAUGH, MARK KRUMEL Designer: MICHAEL TENNYSON SMITH Country: USA
PAGE 6: PHOTOGRAPH BY CARLO ANGELINI Client: MAURO BALMAS CO. Country: ITALY
PAGE 8: Client: MARCEL VAN DER VLUGT Designer: RON VAN DER VLUGT Country: NETHERLANDS

GRAPHIS PUBLICATIONS

GRAPHIS, THE INTERNATIONAL BI-MONTHLY JOURNAL OF VISUAL COMMUNICATION

GRAPHIS DESIGN, THE INTERNATIONAL ANNUAL OF DESIGN AND ILLUSTRATION

GRAPHIS PHOTO, THE INTERNATIONAL ANNUAL OF PHOTOGRAPHY

GRAPHIS POSTER, THE INTERNATIONAL ANNUAL OF POSTER ART

GRAPHIS NUDES, A COLLECTION OF CAREFULLY SELECTED SOPHISTICATED IMAGES

GRAPHIS PACKAGING, AN INTERNATIONAL SURVEY OF PACKAGING DESIGN

GRAPHIS LETTERHEAD, AN INTERNATIONAL SURVEY OF LETTERHEAD DESIGN

GRAPHIS DIAGRAM, THE GRAPHIC VISUALIZATION OF ABSTRACT, TECHNICAL AND STATISTICAL FACTS AND FUNCTIONS

GRAPHIS LOGO, AN INTERNATIONAL SURVEY OF LOGOS

GRAPHIS PUBLICATION, AN INTERNATIONAL SURVEY OF THE BEST IN MAGAZINE DESIGN

GRAPHIS ANNUAL REPORTS, AN INTERNATIONAL COMPILATION OF THE BEST DESIGNED ANNUAL REPORTS

GRAPHIS CORPORATE IDENTITY, AN INTERNATIONAL COMPILATION OF THE BEST IN CORPORATE IDENTITY DESIGN

ART FOR SURVIVAL: THE ILLUSTRATOR AND THE ENVIRONMENT, A DOCUMENT OF ART IN THE SERVICE OF MAN.

THE GRAPHIC DESIGNER'S GREEN BOOK, ENVIRONMENTAL RESOURCES FOR THE DESIGN AND PRINT INDUSTRIES

GRAPHIS PUBLIKATIONEN

GRAPHIS, DIE INTERNATIONALE ZWEIMONATSZEITSCHRIFT DER VISUELLEN KOMMUNIKATION

GRAPHIS DESIGN, DAS INTERNATIONALE JAHRBUCH ÜBER DESIGN UND ILLUSTRATION

GRAPHIS PHOTO, DAS INTERNATIONALE JAHRBUCH DER PHOTOGRAPHIE

GRAPHIS POSTER, DAS INTERNATIONALE JAHRBUCH DER PLAKATKUNST

GRAPHIS NUDES, EINE SAMMLUNG SORGFÄLTIG AUSGEWÄHLTER AKTPHOTOGRAPHIE

GRAPHIS PACKAGING, EIN INTERNATIONALER ÜBERBLICK ÜBER DIE PACKUNGSGESTALTUNG

GRAPHIS LETTERHEAD, EIN INTERNATIONALER ÜBERBLICK ÜBER BRIEFPAPIERGESTALTUNG

GRAPHIS DIAGRAM, DIE GRAPHISCHE DARSTELLUNG ABSTRAKTER TECHNISCHER UND STATISTISCHER DATEN UND FAKTEN

GRAPHIS LOGO, EINE INTERNATIONALE AUSWAHL VON FIRMEN-LOGOS

GRAPHIS MAGAZINDESIGN, EINE INTERNATIONALE ZUSAMMENSTELLUNG DES BESTEN ZEITSCHRIFTEN-DESIGNS

GRAPHIS ANNUAL REPORTS, EIN INTERNATIONALER ÜBERBLICK ÜBER DIE GESTALTUNG VON JAHRESBERICHTEN

GRAPHIS CORPORATE IDENTITY, EINE INTERNATIONALE AUSWAHL DES BESTEN CORPORATE IDENTITY DESIGNS

ART FOR SURVIVAL: THE ILLUSTRATOR AND THE ENVIRONMENT, EIN DOKUMENT ÜBER DIE KUNST IM DIENSTE DES MENSCHEN

THE GRAPHIC DESIGNER'S GREEN BOOK, UMWELTKONZEPTE DER DESIGN- UND DRUCKINDUSTRIE

PUBLICATIONS GRAPHIS

GRAPHIS, LA REVUE BIMESTRIELLE INTERNATIONALE DE LA COMMUNICATION VISUELLE

GRAPHIS DESIGN, LE RÉPERTOIRE INTERNATIONAL DE LA COMMUNICATION VISUELLE

GRAPHIS PHOTO, LE RÉPERTOIRE INTERNATIONAL DE LA PHOTOGRAPHIE

GRAPHIS POSTER, LE RÉPERTOIRE INTERNATIONAL DE L'AFFICHE

GRAPHIS NUDES, UN FLORILEGE DE LA PHOTOGRAPHIE DE NUS

GRAPHIS PACKAGING, LE RÉPERTOIRE INTERNATIONAL DE LA CRÉATION D'EMBALLAGES

GRAPHIS LETTERHEAD, LE RÉPERTOIRE INTERNATIONAL DU DESIGN DE PAPIER À LETTRES

GRAPHIS DIAGRAM, LE RÉPERTOIRE GRAPHIQUE DE FAITS ET DONNÉES ABSTRAITS, TECHNIQUES ET STATISTIQUES

GRAPHIS LOGO, LE RÉPERTOIRE INTERNATIONAL DU LOGO

GRAPHIS PUBLICATION, LE RÉPERTOIRE INTERNATIONAL DU DESIGN DE PÉRIODIQUES

GRAPHIS ANNUAL REPORTS, PANORAMA INTERNATIONAL DU MEILLEUR DESIGN DE RAPPORTS ANNUELS D'ENTREPRISES

GRAPHIS CORPORATE IDENTITY, PANORAMA INTERNATIONAL DU MEILLEUR DESIGN D'IDENTITÉ CORPORATE

ART FOR SURVIVAL: THE ILLUSTRATOR AND THE ENVIRONMENT, L'ART AU SERVICE DE LA SURVIE

THE GRAPHIC DESIGNER'S GREEN BOOK, L'ÉCOLOGIE APPLIQUÉE AU DESIGN ET À L'INDUSTRIE GRAPHIQUE

PUBLICATION NO. 227 (ISBN 3-85709-441.9)

© COPYRIGHT UNDER UNIVERSAL COPYRIGHT CONVENTION

COPYRIGHT © 1993 BY GRAPHIS PRESS CORP., DUFOURSTRASSE 107, 8008 ZURICH, SWITZERLAND

JACKET AND BOOK DESIGN COPYRIGHT © 1993 BY PEDERSEN DESIGN

141 LEXINGTON AVENUE, NEW YORK, N.Y. 10016 USA

CONTENTS · INHALT · SOMMAIRE

REMARKS

WE EXTEND OUR HEARTFELT THANKS TO CONTRIBUTORS THROUGHOUT THE WORLD WHO HAVE MADE IT POSSIBLE TO PUBLISH A WIDE AND INTERNATIONAL SPECTRUM OF THE BEST WORK IN THIS FIELD.

ENTRY INSTRUCTIONS MAY BE REQUESTED AT:
GRAPHIS PRESS CORP.,
DUFOURSTRASSE 107,
8008 ZÜRICH, SWITZERLAND

ANMERKUNGEN

UNSER DANK GILT DEN EINSENDERN AUS ALLER WELT, DIE ES UNS DURCH IHRE BEI-TRÄGE ERMÖGLICHT HABEN, EIN BREITES, INTERNATIONALES SPEKTRUM DER BESTEN ARBEITEN ZU VERÖFFENTLICHEN.

TEILNAHMEBEDINGUNGEN:
GRAPHIS VERLAG AG,
DUFOURSTRASSE 107,
8008 ZÜRICH, SCHWEIZ

ANNOTATIONS

TOUTE NOTRE RECONNAISSANCE VA AUX DESIGNERS DU MONDE ENTIER DONT LES ENVOIS NOUS ONT PERMIS DE CONSTITUER UN VASTE PANORAMA INTERNATIONAL DES MEILLEURES CRÉATIONS.

MODALITÉS D'ENVOI DE TRAVAUX:
EDITIONS GRAPHIS,
DUFOURSTRASSE 107,
8008 ZÜRICH, SUISSE

ERRATA: IN *GRAPHIS LETTERHEAD 1* WE UNFORTUNATELY INCORRECTLY IDENTIFIED THE LETTERHEAD SYSTEM ON PAGE 193 AS BEING DESIGNED AND ART DIRECTED BY KARINA HOLBECK. THAT IN FACT IS THE CLIENT, THE DESIGNER AND ART DIRECTOR IS M. BUGGEREIT. WE REGRET THIS ERROR AND APOLOGIZE TO MR. BUTTGEREIT. ■ **ERRATUM:** IN *GRAPHIS LETTERHEAD 1* HABEN WIR VERSEHENTLICH AUF SEITE 193 FALSCHE KÜNSTLERANGABEN VERÖFFENTLICHT. DAS BRIEFPAPIER FÜR KARINA HOLBECK WURDE VON M. BUTTGEREIT GESTAL-TET. WIR BEDAUERN DIESEN FEHLER AUSSERORDENTLICH UND BITTEN HERRN BUTTGEREIT, DIESES VERSEHEN ZU ENTSCHULDIGEN.

GRAPHIS LETTERHEAD 2

HAS BEEN PRODUCED IN CONJUNCTION WITH

THE "STRATHMORE PRESENTS GRAPHIS" LETTERHEAD EXHIBITION

AND THROUGH THE GENEROUS SUPPORT OF

STRATHMORE PAPER.

GRAPHIS LETTERHEAD 2

WURDE MIT FREUNDLICHER UNTERSTÜTZUNG VON

STRATHMORE PAPER UND IN VERBINDUNG MIT DER AUSSTELLUNG

«STRATHMORE PRESENTS GRAPHIS»

PRODUZIERT.

GRAPHIS LETTERHEAD 2

A ÉTÉ PRODUIT EN COOPÉRATION AVEC

L'EXPOSITION INTITULÉE «STRATHMORE PRESENTS GRAPHIS»

ET GRÂCE AU SOUTIEN GÉNÉREUX DE

STRATHMORE PAPER.

**21 x 29.7
letter**

**22 x 11
envelope**

**6 x 10
business
card**

Marcel van der Vlugt Photography
ADDRESS Oude Looiersstraat 20 – 1016 VJ Amsterdam

Marcel van der Vlugt Photography
ADDRESS Oude Looiersstraat 20 – 1016 VJ Amsterdam
PHONE (020) 622 28 69 FAX (020) 626 48 28

Marcel van der Vlugt Photography
ADDRESS Oude Looiersstraat 20 – 1016 VJ Amsterdam PHONE (020) 622 28 69
FAX (020) 626 48 28 BANK NMB 69 74 85 315 KvK 176 890

COMMENTARIES

KOMMENTARE

COMMENTAIRES

Alan Fletcher

Shortly after accepting an invitation from Graphis to write an article on the design of letterheads, I came to the unnerving conclusion I had little to say that hadn't been said before. After all, I assume those who have bought this handsome and lavishly illustrated publication will learn more about design from looking at the pictures than from my words. However, if the reader wants to know about papers, international sizes, watermarks or printing techniques, then my advice is to buy the first volume of GRAPHIS LETTERHEAD 1. This has an excellent introduction which extensively covers these subjects. □ Over the years, I have sporadically put various pieces of correspondence I have received from designers into a drawer. Looking through them in the vague hope of arriving at a riveting insight to help me do this article, I was surprised at what they revealed. For example, Wolfgang Weingart, agent provocateur of typography, used a typewriter (probably a Remington) to bang out his address, illustrator Bob Blechman tore a sheet out of a graph paper notebook, cartoonist Ralph Steadman favored a rubber stamp. □ Some of the designs were less casual: Jean Michel Folon used diagonally slanted red rules—to accommodate his tilted writing— designed for him, I believe, by Milton Glaser. Certainly only a Polish poster designer would opt to print his address in 16pt Cooper black italic—I'm all for this lack of inhibition. Olivier Mourgue, noted from several letters I kept, always personalizes his notes with a tiny delicately drawn sketch, while Paul Davis turns his envelopes into collages. □ The lesson, I concluded, is this: When it comes to the design of letterheads, the only rule is to avoid rules. ■

ALAN FLETCHER'S INTERNATIONAL DESIGN REPUTATION IS REFLECTED BY HIS COMMISSIONS FROM MAJOR CORPORATIONS AND CULTURAL INSTITUTIONS, WHICH ARE TOO NUMEROUS TO BE LISTED HERE, AS ARE THE MANY AWARDS HE RECEIVED FROM THE MOST PRESTIGIOUS INTERNATIONAL INSTITUTIONS, INCLUDING THE 1993 PRINCE PHILIP PRIZE FOR DESIGNER OF THE YEAR. HE BEGAN HIS CAREER IN NEW YORK WHERE HE WORKED FOR *FORTUNE* MAGAZINE, THE CONTAINER CORPORATION AND IBM. UPON HIS RETURN TO LONDON, HE CO-FOUNDED FLETCHER/ FORBES/GILL IN 1962 AND TEN YEARS LATER PENTAGRAM. IN 1992 HE OPENED HIS OWN STUDIO. ALAN TRAINED AT THE ROYAL COLLEGE OF ART IN LONDON AND THE SCHOOL OF ARCHITECTURE AND DESIGN AT YALE UNIVERSITY.

SAMPLES FROM ALAN FLETCHER'S PERSONAL COLLECTION OF CORRESPONDENCE. (OPENING SPREAD) ENVELOPE BY PAUL DAVIS. (OPPOSITE PAGE, FROM TOP TO BOTTOM AND LEFT TO RIGHT) LETTERS BY JEAN MICHEL FOLON, OLIVIER MOURGUE, WOLFGANG WEINGART, BOB BLECHMAN, RALPH STEADMAN, AND WALDEMAR SWIERZY

Kurz nachdem ich Graphis' Einladung angenommen hatte, einen Beitrag über die Gestaltung von Briefpapier zu schreiben, kam ich zu dem beunruhigenden Schluss, dass ich dem, was bereits über das Thema gesagt worden ist, wenig hinzuzufügen habe. Zudem nehme ich an, dass alle, die dieses zweifellos teure, aber schön und grosszügig illustrierte Buch gekauft haben, von den Abbildungen mehr über Design lernen werden als von meinen Worten. Doch wenn Sie mehr über Papier, internationale Masse, Wasserzeichen und Drucktechnik erfahren möchten, empfehle ich Ihnen, den ersten Band *Graphis Letterhead 1* zu kaufen. Darin finden Sie eine ausgezeichnete Einführung zu diesen Themen. □ Im Laufe der Jahre habe ich immer wieder einige der Briefe, die ich von Designern erhalten hatte, in eine Schublade gelegt. Als ich diese jetzt durchschaute, in der Hoffnung Ideen für diesen Artikel zu finden, war ich erstaunt, was ich fand. Wolfgang Weingart, Agent provocateur der Typographie, benutzt eine Schreib-maschine (wahrscheinlich eine Remington), um seine Adresse herunterzuhauen. Der Illustrator Bob Blechman schrieb seinen Brief auf eine aus einem karierten Block herausgerissene Seite, und der Cartoonist Ralph Steadman benutzt für seine Adresse einen einfachen Gummistempel. □ Andere Designs waren weniger vom Zufall diktiert: Auf Jean Michel Folons Briefpapier befinden sich schräge rote Linien, um seiner schrägen Schrift gerecht zu werden. Ich glaube, sein Briefpapier wurde von Milton Glaser entworfen. Nur ein Plakatkünstler aus Polen kann auf die Idee kommen, seine Adresse in einer 16-Punkt Cooper black kursiv Schrift zu drucken. Bloss keine falsche Bescheidenheit – mir gefällt das. Olivier Mourgue fügt seinen Briefen mit einer kleinen Zeichnung immer etwas Persönliches bei. Und die Couverts von Paul Davis sind die reinsten Collagen. □ Was ich bei dieser Durchsicht gelernt habe, ist dies: Wenn es darum geht, Briefpapier zu entwerfen, gibt es nur eine Regel: Keine Regeln aufzustellen. ■

ALAN FLETCHERS INTERNATIONALER RUF ALS DESIGNER BASIERT AUF SEINEN ARBEITEN FÜR GROSSE UNTERNEHMEN UND KULTURINSTITUTE IN ALLER WELT. DIE LISTE IHRER NAMEN IST SO LANG WIE DIE SEINER AUSZEICHNUNGEN, ER WURDE U.A. 1993 MIT DEM PRINCE PHILIP PREIS ALS DESIGNER DES JAHRES AUSGEZEICHNET. ALAN FLETCHER BEGANN SEINE KARRIERE IN NEW YORK, WO ER FÜR DAS MAGAZIN *FORTUNE*, DIE CONTAINER CORPORATION UND IBM GEARBEITET HAT. ZURÜCK IN LONDON WAR ER 1962 MITBEGRÜNDER VON FLETCHER/FORBES/GILL UND ZEHN JAHRE SPÄTER VON PENTAGRAM. 1992 ERÖFFNETE ER EIN EIGENES STUDIO.

Peu après avoir accepté sur l'invitation de Graphis de rédiger un article sur la conception des en-têtes, j'ai abouti à la conclusion déconcertante que j'avais peu de chose nouvelles à dire sur ce sujet. Je suis d'ailleurs forcé d'admettre que ceux qui ont acheté cette publication indubitablement chère, mais tout à la fois attrayante et somptueusement illustrée, apprendront plus sur le design en regardant les images qu'en lisant ces mots. Toutefois, je conseillerais aux lecteurs qui s'intéressent aux papiers, aux formats internationaux, aux filigranes ou aux techniques d'impression, de faire l'acquisition du premier volume de *Graphis Letterhead 1*. Il contient une excellente introduction qui recouvre l'ensemble du sujet. □ Au fil des ans, j'ai gardé dans un tiroir différents courriers que m'avaient adressés des designers. Lorsque je les ai consultés dans le vague espoir d'obtenir des informations propre à m'aider à rédiger cet article, j'ai été surpris de voir ce qu'ils révélaient. Par exemple, Wolfgang Weingart, agent provocateur typographe, utilisait une machine à écrire (probablement une Remington) pour taper son adresse; l'illustrateur Bob Blechman déchirait une page d'un note-bloc de papier millimétré; le dessinateur Ralph Steadman , lui, préférait le tampon. Certains concepts étaient moins fortuits. Jean Michel Folon se sert de lignes rouges diagonales -j'imagine que Milton Glaser les a dessinées à son attention- pour discipliner son écriture inclinée. Il n'y a qu'un dessinateur d'affiche polonais pour choisir d'imprimer son adresse en caractères Cooper noirs italiques de 16 pt. Personnellement, j'adhère totalement à ce manque d'inhibition. Olivier Mourgue, j'ai pu le vérifier sur plusieurs lettres qui sont en ma possesion, rehausse toujours ses notes d'un petit croquis au dessin délicat, tandis que Paul Davis fait de ses enveloppes des collages. □ La leçon qu'on peut en tirer est que la seule règle en matière de conception des en-têtes est d'éviter toutes les règles. ■

ALAN FLETCHER FAIT SES DÉBUTS À NEW YORK, OÙ IL TRAVAILLE POUR LE MAGAZINE *FORTUNE*, LA CONTAINER CORPORATION ET IBM, PUIS RETOURNE À LONDRES OÙ IL SERA SUCCESSIVEMENT CO-FONDATEUR DE L'AGENCE FLETCHER/FORBES/GILL EN 1962 ET DE PENTAGRAM, DIX ANS PLUS TARD. EN 1992 IL OUVRE SA PROPRE AGENCE. LA RÉPUTATION INTERNATIONALE QUE S'EST ACQUISE LE GRAPHISTE ALAN FLETCHER REPOSE SUR LES RÉALISATIONS QU'IL A EFFECTUÉS POUR LE COMPTE DE GRANDES ENTREPRISES ET D'ORGANISATION CULTURELLES DANS LE MONDE ENTIER. LA LISTE DE SES CLIENTS EST AUSSI LONGUE QUE CELLE DE SES RÉUSSITES.

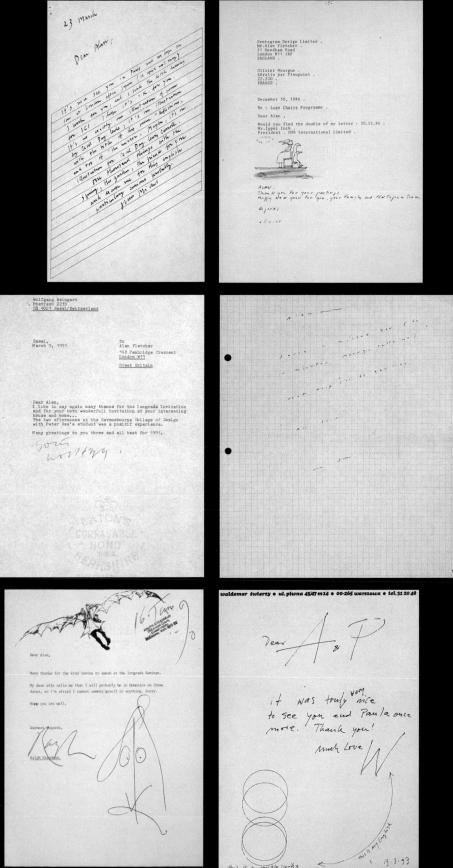

23 March

Dear Alan!

It's nice see you in Paris and we hope see you at London after Japon (10 april → 1 may) I work for you, and I send the little drawing for ICI. I hope it's O.K. for you. It's no exactly one illustration of poem by Cecil Day Lewis, it's one illustration with the title of his poeme "Reflections" and too of "the mirror". Maybe, it's one illustration for Cecil Day Lewis Carroll. One Thousand things with the Spring, the garden, the friends for you and excuse me for this english particulary curious probably.

yours Michel

Pentagram Design Limited .
Mr.Alan Fletcher .
11 Needham Road
London W11 2RP
ENGLAND .

Olivier Mourgue .
Kéralio par Plouguiel .
22.220 .
FRANCE .

December 30, 1986 .

Re : Luge Chairs Programme .

Dear Alan ,

Would you find the double of my letter : 30.12.86 ;
Mr.Ippei Inch .
President . OUN International Limited .

Alan.
Thank you for your greetings
Happy New year for you, your Family and Pentagram Team.

Regards

Olivier

Wolfgang Weingart
Postfach 2235
CH 4001 Basel/Switzerland

Basel,
March 9, 1991

To
Alan Fletcher
14B Pembridge Crescent
London W11

Great Britain

Dear Alan,
I like to say again many thanks for the Icograda Invitation and for your both wonderfull invitation at your interesting house and home...
The two afternoons at the Ravensbourne College of Design with Peter Rea's student was a positif experience.

Many greatings to you three and all best for 1991,

Grüsse
Wolfgang.

Alan —
Sorry I missed you (by 10 minutes.

16. June

RALPH STEADMAN
Old Loose Court,
Loose Valley,
Maidstone, Kent

Dear Alan,

Many thanks for the kind invite to speak at the Icograda Seminar.

My dear wife tells me that I will probably be in Domenica on those dates, so I'm afraid I cannot commit myself to anything. Sorry.

Hopp you are well.

Warmest regards,

Ralph

Ralph Steadman.

waldemar świerzy • ul. piwna 45/47 m14 • 00-265 warszawa • tel. 31 20 48

Dear A & P

it was truly very nice to see you and Paula once more. Thank you!

Much Love

W

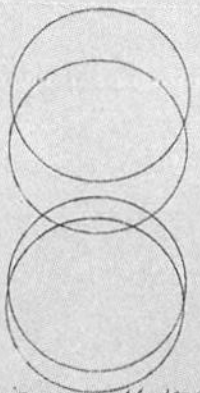

this is a double vodka

this is my English

19.3.93

Sue T. Crolick

I used to think I was too corny to be a designer. □ Designers liked things that were tasteful, cerebral, dignified. □ I liked emotional stuff, visceral stuff, funny stuff. □ I came from the vulgar world of advertising. When I showed up at my first designer party, I was scared. What if they asked me about my past, and I had to say the "A" word? □ That was 8 years ago. I've come a long way since then. Not only have designers accepted me, sometimes they even laugh at my jokes. □ Truth is, in the 12 years since I opened my firm, there's been a fascinating crossover between advertising and design. Ads are showing up with decorative borders full of teeny letterspaced type. And design, thanks to people like Charles Anderson and Paula Scher, has gotten a sense of humor. □ People tell me this crossover shows up a lot in my work. They see it most clearly in my stationery design. □ The traditional graphic design approach to letterheads tells us to be quiet, be conservative, use burgundy, use gray. □ Being an unrecovered agency art director, I had a different point of view. Why disappear when you could be *in their face*? Why bore people with a stuffy little trademark in the corner when you could grab 'em, surprise 'em, delight 'em? Why not treat letterheads like ads? □ Come to think of it, if you're trying to get noticed, maybe letterheads are even better than ads. □ Ads die in six months; corporate identities live for decades. An ad is bordered by a bunch of other ads; a letter is a nice little island. For a moment, held by a captive reader, an 8½"x11" sheet of paper is a true communication opportunity. □ I liked this new angle. I set about trying to take advantage of it. □ Instead of the design approach—abstract symbols—I chose the advertising approach—literal images. Instead of thinking up cool, esoteric visuals, I imagined pictures of warm familiar things, the kind everyone could understand. □ For example, for an architectural firm specializing in residential design, my logo featured the frame of a house built with ordinary, number two pencils (the same pencils the architects used in their renderings). □ Instead of using traditional flat-color line art, I had an ad photographer shoot the image in full color. □ Because most architects present themselves as cool and sophisticated, this firm looked different by appearing warm and friendly. □ For an artists' representative, I resisted flat, emotionless images like the black portfolio. Instead, I "humanized" a drawing board. Artists' reps do a lot of running around. So I added high-heeled shoes to the drawing board's legs, and made the image look real with photography. □ It made people smile. □ For a copywriter specializing in retail, I used the advertising approach again. Her business card looks like a clothing tag, complete with bar code and plastic loop. Her hourly rate of $90 is flagged with a bright yellow "sale price" sticker that shows her reduced rate of $59.99. If she wants to reduce that rate even more, she scratches it out and tells her clients, "For you, this week only, it's $49.99." □ Why did this work? Certainly not because of its elegant design. In fact when I saw the first set of type proofs, I sent them right back. The type didn't look bad enough. □ I think it worked because everyone can relate to a clothing tag; the image is familiar. And the image has an emotional component; it makes people laugh. □ "Yeah, sure," you may be saying to yourself. "That funky human stuff may work for a copywriter, but what about *my* client, Bland and Boring, Incorporated?" □ If you think it's difficult to persuade big companies to humanize their image, you're right. □ But why is this? □ Have we stopped even making an attempt because we, too, buy into the notion that "big company equals dry image?" □ Are we, like that crusty old cigar-chomping corporate boss, afraid a logo with heart could make a company look silly? Or even worse, weak and feminine? □ Okay, I admit it. My credibility as an authentic graphic designer is suspect. I've never done an annual report. I hate capability brochures. I'm definitely not cerebral. I like cartoons and puns (even bad ones). I like reruns of Walt Disney's "Pinocchio" and almost

SUE T. CROLICK ARBEITET ALS ART DIREKTORIN UND DESIGNERIN IN MINNEAPOLIS. IHRE FIRMA WURDE IN *GRAPHIC DESIGN AMERICA, THE WORK OF 28 LEADING EDGE DESIGN FIRMS* VORGESTELLT. SIE HAT GOLDMEDAILLEN VON DER NEW YORK ONE SHOW UND DEM NEW YORK ADC ERHALTEN UND AUSZEICHNUNGEN VON *COMMUNICATION ARTS, GRAPHIS, PRINT* UND A.I.G.A. UND SIE WURDE ZWEIMAL MIT DEM TITEL *BEST OF SHOWS* AUSGEZEICHNET. ARTIKEL ÜBER IHRE ARBEIT SIND IN *COMMUNICATION ARTS* UND *PRINT* ERSCHIENEN. SUE WIRD HÄUFIG ALS GAST-REDNERIN EINGELADEN, UM ÜBER IHRE POSITION ALS ERSTE ART DIREKTORIN VON MINNEAPOLIS ZU SPRECHEN.

anything with a baby picture on it. □ Even allowing for my sentimentality, isn't it still true most design is about as ardent as a stone? □ I'd like to see us designers take a cue from those hokey ad guys and inject more feeling into our work. I want us to help our clients worry less about looking dignified and professional, and more about looking approachable. Let's

declare the abstract coldblooded corporate symbol clinically dead. □ Maybe it's dying already. I've seen hopeful signs lately. □ I've heard that Borden's is bringing back Elsie the cow. And RCA is bringing back its cute little dog. □ So it looks like maybe we'll be seeing more warm fuzzies out there. □ For a corny, sappy, ex-advertising type like me, that's good news. ■

Ich dachte immer, ich sei zu sentimal, um Graphikerin zu werden. □ Designer mögen Sachen, die geschmackvoll, intellektuell, anspruchsvoll sind. □ Ich mag gefühlvolle und lustige Sachen. □ Ich kam aus der vulgären Welt der Werbung. Als ich zum ersten Mal mit Designern zusammenkam,

fühlte ich mich nicht wohl in meiner Haut. Was wäre, wenn sie mich nach meiner Vergangenheit fragten, wenn ich bekennen müsste, woher ich kam. □ Das war vor acht Jahren. Seitdem ist einiges passiert. Die Designer haben mich akzeptiert, sie lachen sogar ab und zu über meine Witze. □ Die

FROM LEFT TO RIGHT: CORPORATE IDENTITES FOR SANDRA HEINEN, INC., THATCHER & THOMPSON, AND JOAN OSTRIN. ■

Wahrheit ist, dass sich in den 12 Jahren seit der Gründung meiner eigenen Firma in der Beziehung zwischen Werbung und Design einiges getan hat. Bei Anzeigen sah man plötzlich dekorative Ränder mit winzigen Buchstaben, und im Design konnte man ein bisschen Humor entdecken, was das Verdienst von Leuten wie Charles Anderson und Paula Scher ist. □ Die Leute behaupten, in meinen Arbeiten viel von dieser gegenseitigen Befruchtung zu sehen. Am deutlichsten sei es bei den Briefköpfen. □ Die herkömmliche Vorstellung

von Briefpapier lässt den Designer an etwas Ruhiges, Konservatives mit Weinrot und Grau denken. □ Als unverbesserliche Art Direktorin einer Agentur war ich anderer Ansicht. Warum so zurückhaltend sein? Warum die Leute mit einem winzigen Firmenzeichen in der Ecke langweilen, wenn man sie packen, sie überraschen, erfreuen kann? Warum soll man Briefköpfe nicht wie Anzeigen behandeln? □ Wenn man es sich genau überlegt, sind Briefköpfe vielleicht sogar besser als Anzeigen, wenn man Aufmerksamkeit will. □ Anzeigen

S U E   T.   C R O L I C K   ARBEITET ALS ART DIREKTORIN UND DESIGNERIN IN MINNEAPOLIS. IHRE FIRMA WURDE IN GRAPHIC DESIGN AMERICA, THE WORK OF 28 LEADING EDGE DESIGN FIRMS VORGESTELLT. SIE HAT GOLDMEDAILLEN VON DER NEW YORK ONE SHOW UND DEM NEW YORK ADC ERHALTEN UND AUSZEICHNUNGEN VON COMMUNICATION ARTS, GRAPHIS, PRINT UND A.I.G.A. UND SIE WURDE ZWEIMAL MIT DEM TITEL BEST OF SHOWS AUSGEZEICHNET. ARTIKEL ÜBER IHRE ARBEIT SIND IN COMMUNICATION ARTS UND PRINT ERSCHIENEN. SUE WIRD HÄUFIG ALS GASTREDNERIN EINGELADEN, UM ÜBER IHRE POSITON ALS ERSTE ART DIREKTORIN VON MINNEAPOLIS ZU SPRECHEN.

sterben in sechs Monaten, Erscheinungsbilder leben jahrzehntelang. Eine Anzeige hat sich gegen eine Menge anderer Anzeigen durchzusetzen; ein Brief ist eine schöne kleine Insel für sich. In der Hand eines aufmerksamen Lesers wird er für einen Moment zu einer echten Kommunikationsmöglichkeit. □ Mir gefiel dieser Gesichtspunkt, und ich machte ihn mir zunutze. □ Statt der im Design üblichen abstrakten Symbole wählte ich die Sprache der Werbung: realistische Bilder. Ich dachte an warme, vertraute Dinge, die jeder verstehen kann. □ Mein Logoentwurf für ein auf Wohnhäuser spezialisiertes Architekturbüro bestand aus den Umrissen eines Hauses, die von Bleistiften geformt wurden, und zwar von der Sorte, die Architekten für ihre Skizzen verwenden. □ Statt die übliche Strichvorlage im Vollton zu liefern, liess ich das Bild von einem Werbephotographen farbig aufnehmen. □ Diese Firma setzte sich klar von der Konkurrenz ab. Sie gab sich nicht kühl und intellektuell wie die meisten Architekten, ihr Auftritt war warm und freundlich. □ Für eine Künstleragentur machte ich statt der üblichen langweiligen Bilder wie schwarze Präsentationsmappen ein sehr menschliches Zeichenbrett. Agenten sind viel unterwegs, also versah ich die Beine des Zeichentisches mit hochhackigen Schuhen und photographierte das Bild, damit es real wirkt. □ Es brachte die Leute zum Schmunzeln. □ Für eine Texterin, die sich auf den Einzelhandel spezialisiert hat, ging ich wieder wie ein Werbeprofi vor. Ihre Visitenkarte sieht wie ein Preisetikett für Kleider aus, komplett mit Computercode und Plastikschlaufe. Über ihrem Stundensatz von $90.– prangt ein leuchtend gelber Sonderpreis-Aufkleber mit einem reduzierten Preis von $59.99. Wenn sie noch tiefer gehen will, streicht sie ihn durch und gibt ihren Kunden den speziellen neuen Sonderrabatt an. □ Warum hat das funktioniert? Bestimmt nicht wegen des eleganten De-

signs. Ich habe sogar die ersten Abzüge zurückgeschickt, weil die Schrift nicht hässlich genug aussah. □ Ich glaube, es funktionierte, weil jedermann Kleideranhänger kennt, das Bild ist vertraut, und es hat eine emotionale Komponente: Die Leute können darüber lachen. □ «Klar», sagen Sie vielleicht, «bei einer Texterin kann man wohl solche Sachen machen, aber was ist mit meinem langweiligen, nichtssagenden Kunden?» □ Sie haben recht. Es ist schwer, grosse Firmen davon zu überzeugen, ihr Erscheinungsbild menschlicher zu machen. □ Aber warum ist das so? □ Haben wir es aufgegeben, überhaupt einen Versuch zu machen, weil selbst wir überzeugt sind, dass der Auftritt einer grossen Firma nüchtern zu sein hat. □ Sind wir wie der mürrische, Zigarren qualmende, alte Firmenchef, der befürchtet, dass die Firma durch ein Logo mit Herz lächerlich oder, was noch schlimmer wäre, weich und feminin wirken würde? □ O.k. ich gebe es zu. Als Graphikerin bin ich unglaubwürdig. Ich habe noch nie einen Jahresbericht gemacht, ich hasse Firmenbroschüren, und ich bin absolut nicht intellektuell. Ich mag Cartoons und Wortspiele (sogar schlechte). Ich liebe Walt Disneys Film *Pinocchio* und so ziemlich alles, auf dem ein Baby abgebildet ist. □ Auch wenn ich vielleicht sentimental bin – stimmt es etwa nicht, dass das meiste Design so leidenschaftlich wie ein Stein ist? □ Ich wünschte, dass wir Graphiker uns von den verrückten Werbeleuten anstecken liessen und mehr Gefühl in unsere Arbeit legten. Wir sollten unsere Kunden davon überzeugen, dass sie sich nicht unbedingt würdevoll und professionell geben müssen, sondern vor allem zugänglich. Das abstrakte, kaltblütige Firmensymbol sollte endlich für klinisch tot erklärt werden. □ Vielleicht stirbt es bereits. Ich habe kürzlich ermutigende Anzeichen dafür bemerkt. □ Für eine sentimentale, verspielte Ex-Werbefrau wie mich sind das gute Nachrichten. ■

J'étais toujours persuadée d'être trop excentrique pour être graphiste. □ Les graphistes apprécient ce qui est beau, sobre, intellectuel. Moi, j'ai toujours aimé les trucs plutôt drôles, qui provoquent l'émotion. □ Et pour cause! je suis issue du monde «vulgaire» de la publicité. Lorsque j'ai paru pour la première fois à une soirée entre graphistes, j'étais folle d'angoisse. Et si l'on me questionnait sur mes antécédents et si je devais avouer que j'étais une «fille de pub»? C'était il y a 8 ans déjà. J'ai fait beaucoup de chemin depuis. Non seulement les graphistes m'ont acceptés dans leur monde, mais il leur arrive même de rire de mes plaisanteries! □ La vérité, c'est que dans les douze dernières années,

depuis l'ouverture de mon agence, il s'est produit une fascinante osmose entre la publicité et le graphisme. L'on découvre des publicités enchâssées dans un cadre composé de minuscules caractères d'imprimerie, quant au graphisme, il a découvert les vertus de l'humour grâce à des artistes comme Charles Anderson et Paula Scher. □ Les gens me disent que mon travail se ressent de cette filiation publicitaire, en particulier mes graphismes pour papeteries. □ L'approche graphique traditionnelle pour le papier à entête se veut élégante, distinguée, n'utilisant que des couleurs discrètes comme le gris et le rouge bordeaux. □ Comme je ne me suis jamais guérie de mon passé publicitaire, je défends un point de vue opposé. Pourquoi tant de retenue, lorsqu'un papier à entête donne précisément l'occasion de «taper dans l'oeil» du client? Pourquoi une entête banale alors qu'on a justement la possibilité de captiver et de séduire le destinataire? Enfin, pourquoi ne pas considérer le papier à lettres comme de la «pub douce»? ☐ Lorsqu'on y pense, le papier à lettres peut être une manière particulièrement subtile de «faire de la pub» sans en avoir l'air. ☐ Une publicité a une durée de vie de 6 mois au maximum. L'identité institutionnelle, elle, vit durant plusieurs décennies. Une publicité a le désavantage d'être noyée dans le contexte de la concurrence, tandis qu'une lettre a le privilège de capter entièrement l'attention du lecteur durant plusieurs minutes. L'entête représente donc une occasion unique de communiquer un message. ☐ Cette particularité m'a tout de suite intéressée et depuis, je me suis efforcée d'en tirer le meilleur parti. ☐ Contrairement à l'approche graphique, qui utilise des symboles abstraits, j'ai choisi l'approche publicitaire, qui est entièrement visuelle. Plutôt que de créer des formes ésotérique, j'ai décidé d'employer des images familières, qui soient à la portée de tout le monde. ☐ Par exemple, pour un bureau d'architecte spécialisé dans les projets d'immeubles résidentiels, j'ai imaginé un sigle représentant la structure d'une maison formée par des crayons, ceux-là mêmes qu'utilisent quotidiennement les architectes. ☐ Plutôt que d'utiliser un original au trait en teinte complète, j'ai demandé à un photographe d'en prendre une photo couleur. ☐ Comme la plupart des bureaux d'architectes projettent une image froide et sérieuse, celui-ci se distinguait de ses concurrents en présentant une image chaleureuse et amicale. ☐ Dans le cas d'une agence artistique, au lieu d'utiliser la représentation du traditionnel cartable noir, j'ai «humanisé» la planche à dessin. Les agents sont souvent en route, c'est pourquoi je lui ai donné des jambes pourvues de talons aiguilles et j'ai fait photographier le tout pour lui donner l'air réel. ☐ Pour une rédactrice publicitaire, spécialisé dans le commerce de détail, j'ai créé une carte de visite ressemblant à une étiquette de prix (compris code bar et bague plastique). Juxtaposée à son tarif horaire de $90, une étiquette fluo indiquait le «prix barré» de $59,99. Si elle souhaitait réduire encore ce tarif, il lui suffisait de le tracer et d'indiquer à son client qu'elle lui faisait une faveur particulière à $49.99». ☐ Pourquoi est-ce que cela a marché? Certainement pas parce que le design était élégant! En fait lorsque j'ai vu les premières épreuves, je les ai renvoyées immédiatement: la typographie n'était pas assez vulgaire! ☐ Je crois que la raison pour laquelle ça a marché, c'est parce que tout un chacun sait ce qu'est une étiquette de prix. L'image véhicule une charge émotionnelle, elle fait rire les gens. ☐ «Ouais, vous direz-vous, ce genre de trucs, ça joue peut-être pour une rédactrice publicitaire, mais certainement pas en ce qui concerne mon client.» ☐ Si vous pensez qu'il est difficile d'amener les grosses entreprises à humaniser leur image, vous avez raison. ☐ Mais pourquoi cela? Serions-nous nous-mêmes convaincus, en définitive, qu'une grande entreprise doit présenter une image aussi sèche qu'ennuyeuse? Sommes-nous comme ce patron vieux-jeux qui craint qu'un logo ayant du coeur fasse du tord à l'entreprise? Qu'il lui donne l'air bêbête, ou même pire, projette une image dégénérée et «féminine»? ☐ OK, j'avoue que ma crédibilité en tant que graphiste n'est pas au-dessus de tous soupçons. Je n'ai jamais fait un rapport annuel de ma vie, je déteste les brochures institutionnelles, bref, je suis une anti-cérébrale! J'aime les BD et les jeux de mots (même mauvais!). J'aime les films de Walt Disney et tout ce qui se rapporte au monde des bébés. ☐ Même si vous me trouvez excessivement sentimentale, vous m'accorderez que le graphisme est généralement parfaitement démuni d'émotion. ☐ J'aimerais voir les graphistes prendre exemple sur ces dingues de publicitaires, les voir injecter un peu plus de sentiment dans leur travail. Nous devrions convaincre nos clients qu'il n'est pas obligatoire d'avoir l'air digne et grave pour être professionnel, et qu'ils devraient plutôt se préoccuper de créer une plus grande proximité psychologique avec leur public. ☐ Le mieux serait encore de déclarer le «symbolisme institutionnel» mort et enterré. D'ailleurs il est bien possible qu'il soit déjà mort. Certains signes ne trompent pas. ☐ J'ai appris que Borden a redonné vie à Elsie la Vache et que RCA a réintroduit le sigle du petit chien. ☐ Enfin, il semble que des mascottes amusantes vont faire leur réapparition dans le paysage. ☐ Pour une publicitaire non repentie comme je le suis, c'est une bonne nouvelle! ∎

SUE CROLICK EST DIRECTRICE ARTISTIQUE ET GRAPHISTE À MINNEAPOLIS. SON AGENCE EST PRÉSENTÉE DANS LA PUBLICATION *GRAPHIC DESIGN AMERICA, THE WORK OF 28 LEADING EDGE DESIGN FIRMS*. SUE CROLICK A ÉTÉ L'OBJET DE NOMBREUSES DISTINCTIONS. ELLE A ENTRE AUTRES REÇU LE PRIX DU NEW YORK ONE SHOW ET DU NEW YORK ART DIRECTORS CLUB, AINSI QUE D'AUTRES RÉCOMPENSES DE *COMMUNICATION ARTS, GRAPHIS, PRINT* ET A.I.G.A. ELLE A ÉGALEMENT OBTENU DEUX FOIS LE "BEST OF SHOW" DU SHOW DE MINNEAPOLIS. DES ARTICLES SUR SON TRAVAIL DE CRÉATION ONT PARU DANS LES PUBLICATIONS *COMMUNICATION ARTS* AND *PRINT*. SUE CROLICK, PREMIÈRE FEMME DIRECTRICE ARTISTIQUE D'AGENCE À MINNEAPOLIS, DONNE ÉGALEMENT RÉGULIÈREMENT DES CONFÉRENCES SUR SON TRAVAIL DE GRAPHISTE.

CREATIVE SERVICES

KREATIVE DIENSTE

SERVICES CRÉATIFS

CLIENT: DAVID PAUL SAMPSON
ART DIRECTOR/DESIGNER: DAN RICHARDS
COUNTRY: USA

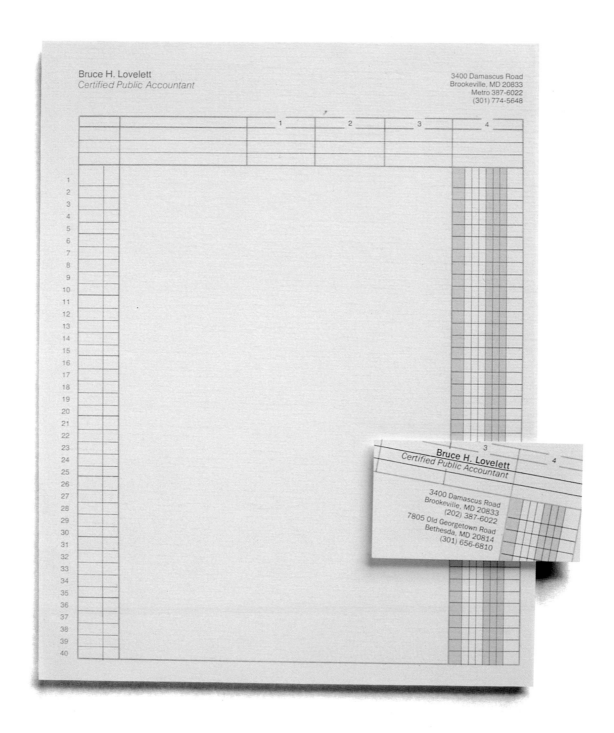

CLIENT: BRUCE H. LOVELETT

DESIGN FIRM: BREMMER & GORIS

ART DIRECTOR: DENNIS GORIS

DESIGNER: MELINDA BREMMER

COUNTRY: USA

CLIENT: BEATE WELLER
DESIGN FIRM: MODERNE REKLAME
ART DIRECTORS/DESIGNERS: KARL MÜLLER, GABI KOLOSS-MÜLLER
COUNTRY: GERMANY

CLIENT: KEHRT SHATKEN SHARON ARCHITECTS
DESIGN FIRM: COOK AND SHANOSKY ASSOC., INC.
ART DIRECTORS/DESIGNERS: ROGER COOK, DON SHANOSKY
COUNTRY: USA

CLIENT: WIEDERKEHR + ZAMPIERI
DESIGN FIRM: ATELIER GIOVANNINI
ART DIRECTOR: PETER GIOVANNINI
COUNTRY: SWITZERLAND

CLIENT: SALIN ASSOCIATES
DESIGN FIRM: JON WELLS ASSOCIATES
DESIGNER: JON WELLS
COUNTRY: USA

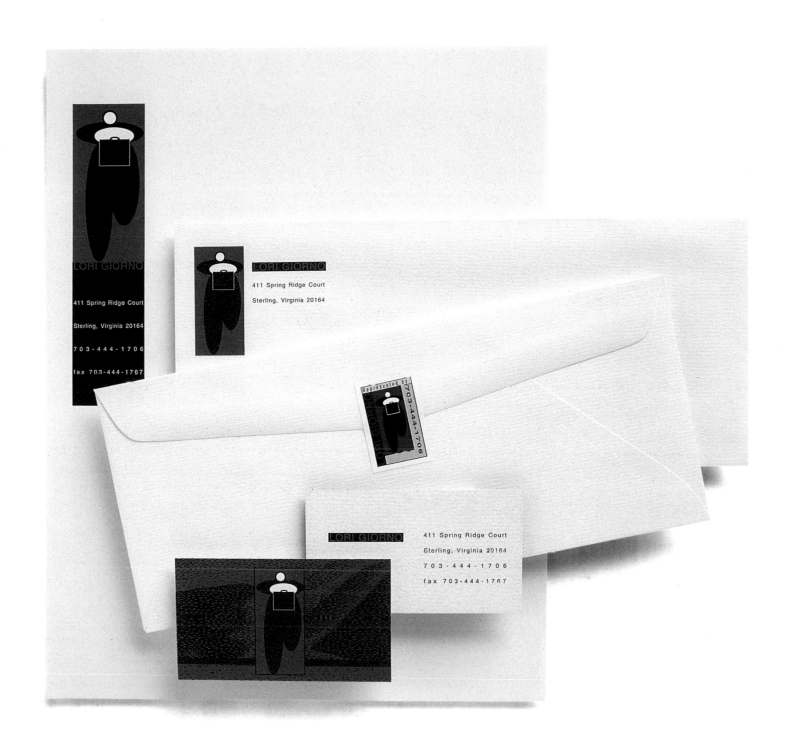

CLIENT: LORI GIORNO
DESIGN FIRM: CHRIS NOEL DESIGN, INC.
ART DIRECTOR/DESIGNER: CHRIS NOEL
ILLUSTRATOR: CHRIS NOEL
COUNTRY: USA

Client: SCHUMANN & COMPANY
Design Firm: DEARWATER DESIGN
Art Director: ANDY DEARWATER
Country: USA

Agent Incorporated

Agent Incorporated

Mary Meehan

Agent Incorporated
2407 Girard Avenue South
Minneapolis, Minnesota 55405
(612) 377-2519
Fax (612) 377-8168

Product Development, Private Label, Licensing

2407 Girard Avenue South
Minneapolis, Minnesota 55405
(612) 377-2519, Fax(612) 377-8168

Product Development, Private Label, Licensing

CLIENT: AGENT INCORPORATED
DESIGN FIRM: DESIGN GUYS
ART DIRECTOR: STEVEN SIKORA
DESIGNER: CATHERINE KNAEBLE
COUNTRY: USA

THE
SCRUTINY
COMPANY

THE
SCRUTINY
COMPANY

MARTIN MENDOZA

THE SCRUTINY COMPANY LTD
33 WELBECK STREET
LONDON W1M 7PG
TELEPHONE 071 872 0023
FAX 071 872 0024/5 OR 081 201 8262

THE SCRUTINY COMPANY LTD
33 WELBECK STREET · LONDON W1M 7PG
TELEPHONE 071 872 0023
FAX 071 872 0024/5 OR 081 201 8262

DIRECTORS · A.S. ORTON · M. MENDOZA

REGISTERED IN ENGLAND NUMBER 271 4532 · REGISTERED OFFICE · AS ABOVE

CLIENT: THE SCRUTINY COMPANY LTD.
DESIGN FIRM: FORWARD PUBLISHING
ART DIRECTOR/DESIGNER: WILLIAM SCOTT
COUNTRY: GREAT BRITAIN

CLIENT: BRADLEY GROUP
DESIGN FIRM: MARGO CHASE DESIGN
ART DIRECTOR/DESIGNER: MARGO CHASE
COUNTRY: USA

Client: KEITH SCHNELL
Design Firm: PEDERSEN GESK
Art Director/Designer: MITCHELL LINDGREN
Country: USA

CLIENT: GOOD PICTURES

DESIGN FIRM: MORLA DESIGN

ART DIRECTOR: JENNIFER MORLA

DESIGNERS: JENNIFER MORLA, SHARRIE BROOKS

COUNTRY: USA

CINERGI PRODUCTIONS INC.
414 North Camden Drive, 10th Floor
Beverly Hills, California 90210

CINERGI

CINERGI PRODUCTIONS INC., 414 North Camden Drive, 10th Floor
Beverly Hills, California 90210 Tel (213) 859-0331 Fax (213) 859-1092

CINERGI PRODUCTIONS INC., 414 North Camden Drive, 10th Floor, Beverly Hills, California 90210   Tel (213) 859-0331 Fax (213) 859-1092

CLIENT: CINERGI PRODUCTIONS INC.
DESIGN FIRM: ROD DYER GROUP, INC.
ART DIRECTOR: ROD DYER
DESIGNER: STEVE TWIGGER
COUNTRY: USA

Client: RED SKY FILM
Designer: MICHAEL SCHWAB DESIGN
Illustrator: MICHAEL SCHWAB
Country: USA

CLIENT: C PICTURES
DESIGN FIRM: PETERSON & COMPANY
ART DIRECTOR/DESIGNER: BRYAN L. PETERSON
COUNTRY: USA

ONE OF THOSE DAYS

XYZ Productions
2727 Saint Paul Street
Baltimore, MD 21218
301 889 5852

Sean Connolly

**ONE
OF
THOSE
DAYS**

XYZ Productions
2727 Saint Paul Street
Baltimore, MD 21218
301 889 5852

**ONE
OF
THOSE
DAYS**

XYZ Productions
2727 Saint Paul Street
Baltimore, MD 21218
301 889 5852

Sean Connolly

CLIENT: ONE OF THOSE DAYS
DESIGN FIRM: FRANK D'ASTOLFO DESIGN
ART DIRECTOR/DESIGNER: FRANK D'ASTOLFO
COUNTRY: USA

CLIENT: MOVIE TUNES

ART DIRECTOR/DESIGNER: MARILYN FRANDSEN

COUNTRY: USA

Mark Wright
Production Services

802 Revere Drive
Sunnyvale, California 94087

Mark Wright
Production Services

802 Revere Drive
Sunnyvale, California
94087

Phone 408. 737. 8011
Fax 408. 732. 5455

Mark Wright
Production Services

802 Revere Drive
Sunnyvale, California 94087

Phone 408. 737. 8011
Fax 408. 732. 5455

CLIENT: MARK WRIGHT
DESIGN FIRM: STEPHEN SIELER DESIGN
ART DIRECTOR/DESIGNER: STEPHEN SIELER
ILLUSTRATOR: STEPHEN SIELER
COUNTRY: USA

CLIENT: BELL RADIO & TELEVISION
DESIGN FIRM: R.O. BLECHMAN, INC.
ART DIRECTOR/DESIGNER: R.O. BLECHMAN
ILLUSTRATOR: R.O. BLECHMAN
COUNTRY: USA

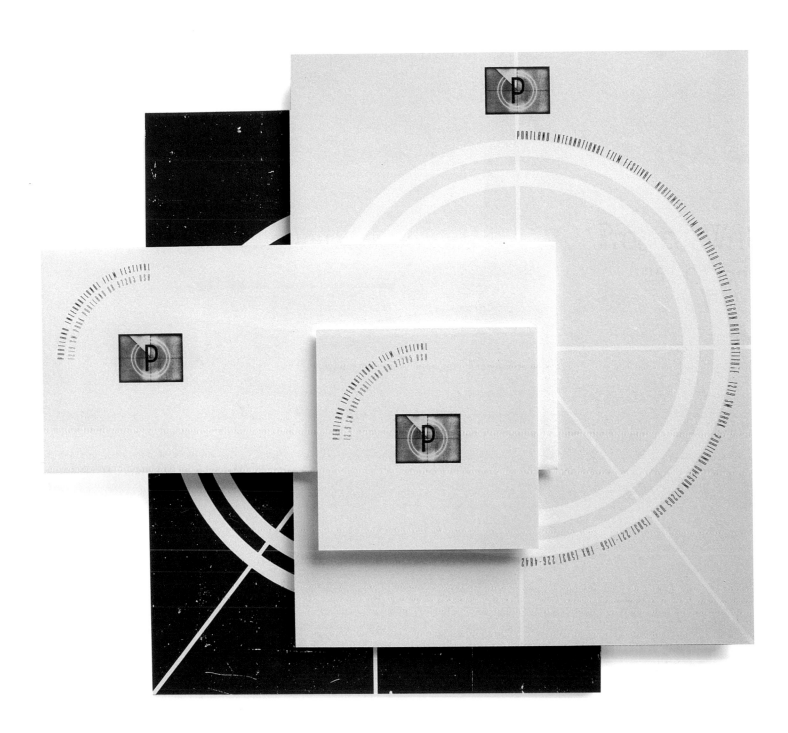

CLIENT: OREGON ART INSTITUTE
DESIGN FIRM: SANDSTROM DESIGN
DESIGNER: STEVE SANDSTROM
ARTIST: GREG KROLICKI
COUNTRY: USA

FILM EDITOR

TOD FEUERMAN

FILM EDITOR

14739 HUSTON STREET

SHERMAN OAKS CA 91403

818.990.7224

FILM EDITOR

FILM EDITOR

TOD FEUERMAN

FILM EDITOR

14739 HUSTON STREET

SHERMAN OAKS CA 91403

818.990.7224

FILM EDITOR

CLIENT: TOD FEUERMAN

DESIGN FIRM: CHERMAYEFF & GEISMAR INC.

DESIGN DIRECTOR/DESIGNER: STEFF GEISSBUHLER

COUNTRY: USA

Client: NONSUCH FILMS
Design Firm: PENTAGRAM
Art Director: WOODY PIRTLE
Designer: JENNIFER LONG
Country: USA

SİNESKOP
FİLM
TELEVİZYON
YAPIM VE
TANITIM
HİZMETLERİ
LİMİTED
ŞİRKETİ

sineskop

ABİDE-İ HÜRRİYET CADDESİ
MECİDİYEKÖY İŞ MERKEZİ
KAT 11, DAİRE 16
MECİDİYEKÖY, İSTANBUL
TELEFON 288 1493
FAKS 346 3090

sineskop

SİNESKOP
FİLM
TELEVİZYON
YAPIM VE
TANITIM
HİZMETLERİ
LİMİTED
ŞİRKETİ

HALİL GÜNGÖR

ABİDE-İ HÜRRİYET CADDESİ
MECİDİYEKÖY İŞ MERKEZİ
KAT 11, DAİRE 16
MECİDİYEKÖY, İSTANBUL
TELEFON 288 14913
FAKS 346 3090

CLIENT: SINESKOP

ART DIRECTOR/DESIGNER: BÜLENT ERKMEN

ILLUSTRATOR: BÜLENT ERKMEN

COUNTRY: TURKEY

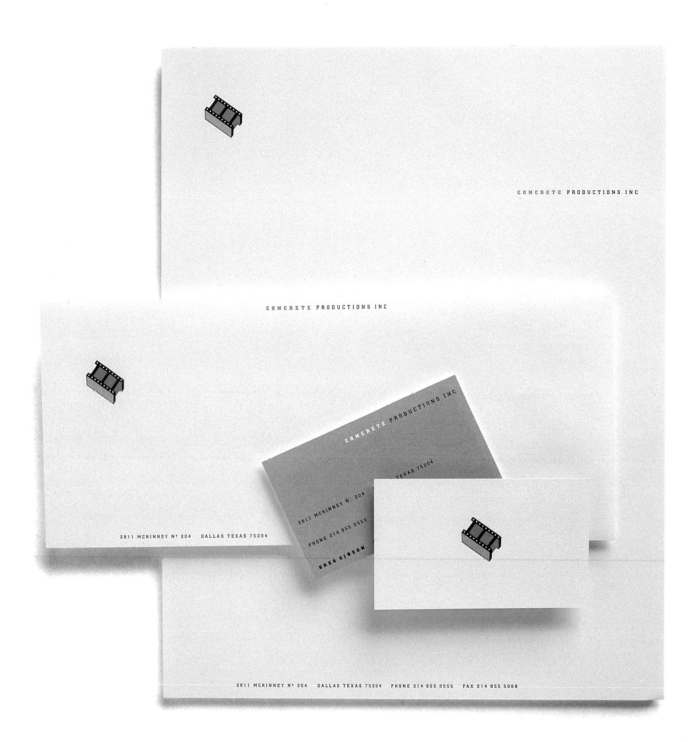

CLIENT: CONCRETE PRODUCTIONS INC.
DESIGN FIRM: PETERSON & COMPANY
ART DIRECTOR: BRYAN L. PETERSON
DESIGNER: SCOTT FEASTER
COUNTRY: USA

CLIENT: TOMAS ANDRÉASSON
DESIGNER: TOMAS ANDRÉASSON
COUNTRY: SWEDEN

CLIENT: ADVICO YOUNG & RUBICAM
DESIGN FIRM: ADVICO YOUNG & RUBICAM
ART DIRECTOR: ROLAND SCOTONI
ARTIST: ALAN FLETCHER
COUNTRY: SWITZERLAND

ART DIRECTOR: ULF NAWROT

ILLUSTRATOR: ULF NAWROT

COUNTRY: GERMANY

221 WEST MAPLE AVENUE • MONROVIA CALIFORNIA 91016

TEL 818 303-5135 • FAX 818 303-1123

CLIENT: MARK RYDEN
DESIGN FIRM: MARK RYDEN ILLUSTRATION
ART DIRECTOR/DESIGNER: MARK RYDEN
ILLUSTRATOR: MARK RYDEN
COUNTRY: USA

CLIENT: WALTER PFENNINGER
DESIGN FIRM: WALTER PFENNINGER
ART DIRECTOR/DESIGNER: WALTER PFENNINGER
ILLUSTRATOR: WALTER PFENNINGER
COUNTRY: SWITZERLAND

CLIENT: BOULETTE BOUTIQUE
DESIGN FIRM: CARTON-BLEU
ILLUSTRATOR: MARIE PAULE ANTOINE
COUNTRY: FRANCE

tauthaus music
Oranienplatz 4, 1000 Berlin 36
Telefon 030-615 31 98, Fax 030-614 50 78

tauthaus music is a division of
Projektateliers für Mediengestaltung,
-konzeption und -produktion GmbH & Co. KG

CLIENT: TAUTHAUS MUSIC

DESIGN FIRM: PROJEKTATELIERS GMBH

ART DIRECTOR/DESIGNER: ROMAN RUSKA

ILLUSTRATOR: ROMAN RUSKA

COUNTRY: GERMANY

In residence at
Blackheath Concert Halls
23 Lee Road
London SE3 9RQ
Tel 081 852 1295
Fax 081 852 5154

Endymion Ensemble

Endymion Ensemble
In residence at
Blackheath Concert Halls

Influences
Three music days
of Brahms and Schönberg
introduced by Robert Saxton.

In residence at
Blackheath Concert Halls
23 Lee Road
London SE3 9RQ
Tel 081 852 1295
Fax 081 852 5154

Endymion Ensemble Ltd
Company No 1783672
Charity No 288788
Vat Reg No 466 323248

Carol Butler
Endymion Ensemble

CLIENT: ENOYMION ENSEMBLE
DESIGN FIRM: PENTAGRAM DESIGN
ART DIRECTOR: JOHN RUSHWORTH
DESIGNERS: JOHN RUSHWORTH, VINCE FROST
COUNTRY: GREAT BRITAIN

New York Theatre

144 West 27th Street
Suite 12
New York NY 10001
212.206.7009

Group Members
Kathleen Mary /Artistic Director
Elizabeth Rosa Arnold
Scott Cargle
Amy Wheeler

New York Theatre

144 West 27th Street
Suite 12
New York NY 10001
212.206.7009

144 West 27th Street
Suite 12
New York NY 10001
212.206.7009

New York Theatre

Client: NEW YORK THEATRE

Design Firm: VICTORE DESIGN WORKS

Designer: JAMES VICTORE

Country: USA

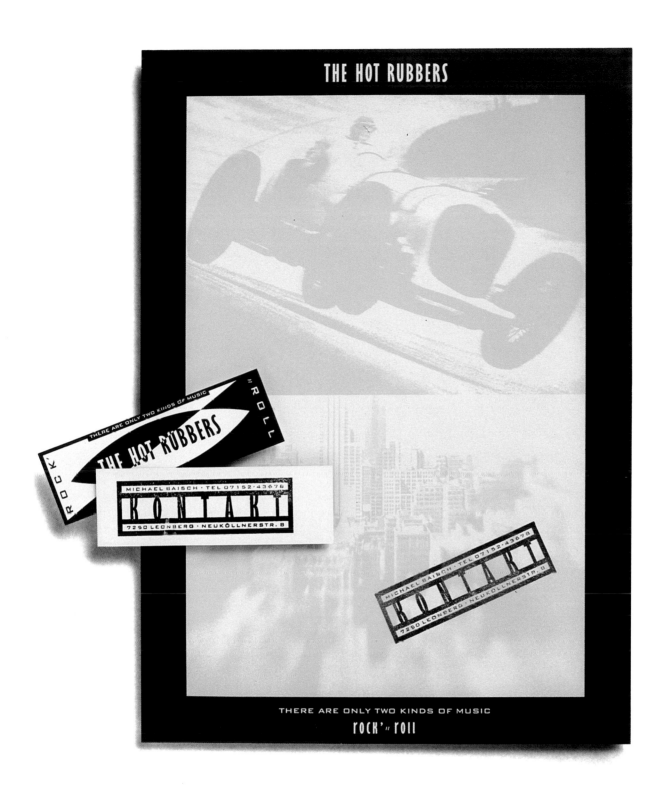

Client: THE HOT RUBBERS
Design Firm: JOERG BAUER DESIGN
Art Director/Designer: JOERG BAUER
Country: GERMANY

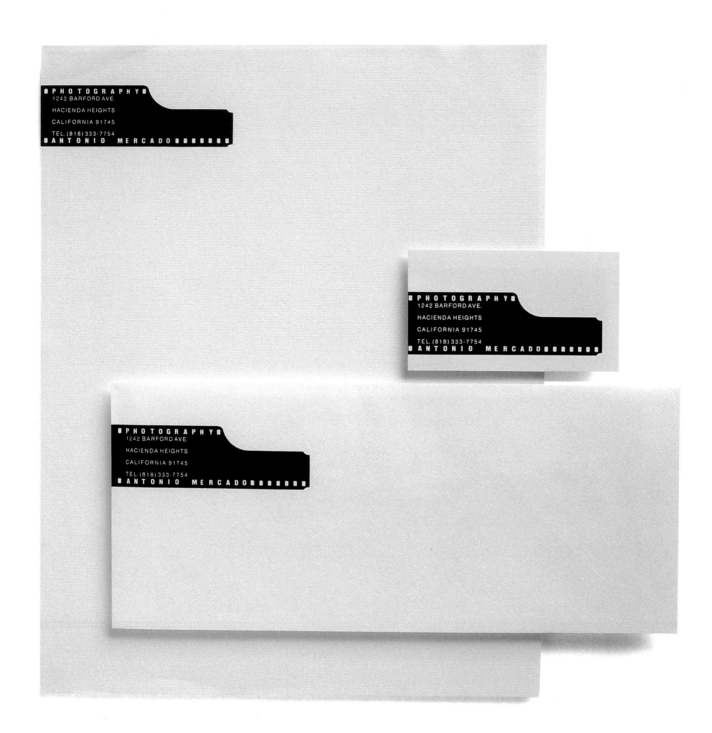

Client: ANTONIO MERCADO PHOTOGRAPHY
Design Firm: MIRES DESIGN, INC.
Art Director/Designer: JOSE SERRANO
Country: USA

CLIENT: ALWIN GREYSON PHOTOGRAPHY
DESIGN FIRM: SCOPE CREATIVE MARKETING
ART DIRECTOR/DESIGNER: DARLENE DALEY
COUNTRY: GREAT BRITAIN

BRIGITTE RICHTER FOTÓGRAFA ■ c/. QUADRADO 9 · 07100 SOLLER (MALLORCA)
TELEFONO 0034.71.632299 · TELEFAX 633217 · APARTADO DE CORREOS 183
ALEMANIA ■ c/o CHRISTA KLUBERT · TEL. 0211.5570606 · FAX 0211.554008

CLIENT: BRIGITTE RICHTER
DESIGN FIRM: CLAUS KOCH
ART DIRECTOR/DESIGNER: CLAUS KOCH
ILLUSTRATOR: CHRISTINE HABERSTOCK
COUNTRY: SPAIN

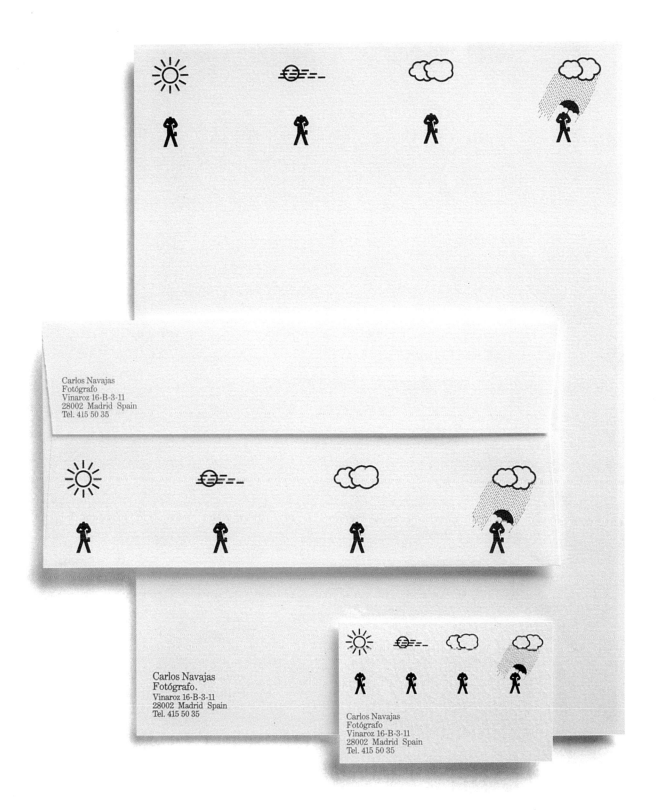

CLIENT: CARLOS NAVAJAS

DESIGN FIRM: TRIOM DESIGN

DESIGNER: FERNANDO MEDINA

ILLUSTRATOR: FERNANDO MEDINA

COUNTRY: SPAIN

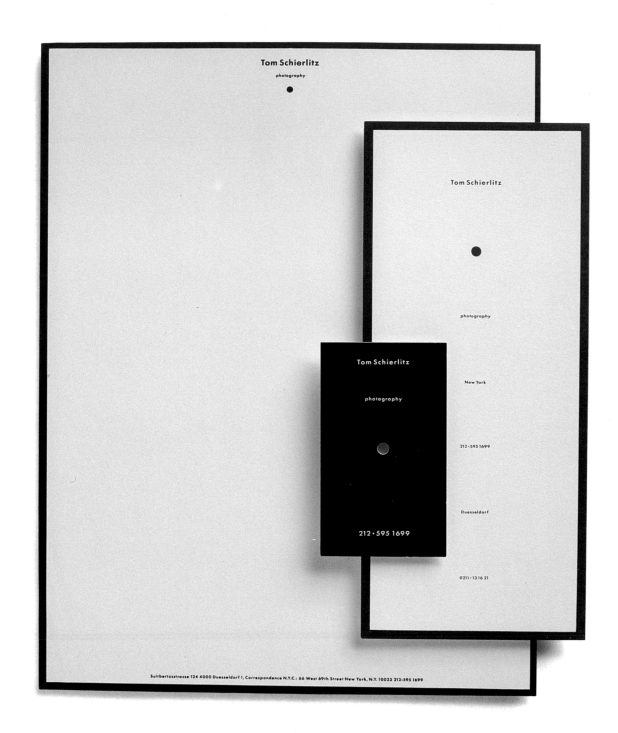

CLIENT: THOMAS SCHIERLITZ
DESIGN FIRM: SAGMEISTER GRAPHICS
ART DIRECTOR/DESIGNER: STEFAN SAGMEISTER
COUNTRY: GERMANY/USA

Michael Furman Photographer

Michael Furman Photographer

Telephone
212. 873. 4417
Facsimile
212. 874. 0831

Elaine Sorel
640 West End Avenue
Suite 8A
New York, New York
10024

Michael Furman Photographer

Telephone
215. 925. 4233
Facsimile
215. 925. 6108

115 Arch Street
Philadelphia,
Pennsylvania
19106

Victoria Satterthwaite

CLIENT: MICHAEL FURMAN PHOTOGRAPHY
DESIGN FIRM: POLITE DESIGN
DESIGNER: KERRY POLITE
COUNTRY: USA

R O B B   M U R R A Y   &   C O M P A N Y

R O B B   M U R R A Y   &   C O M P A N Y

FINE SCREEN PRINTING · 1546 WALLACE SAN FRANCISCO CALIFORNIA 94124 TEL 415. 822.1222 FAX 415.822.1229

CLIENT: ROBB MURRAY & COMPANY
DESIGN FIRM: VANDERBYL DESIGN
ART DIRECTOR/DESIGNER: MICHAEL VANDERBYL
ILLUSTRATOR: MICHAEL VANDERBYL
COUNTRY: USA

CLIENT: EXPRESS QUALITY PRINTING INC.

DESIGN FIRM: TOLLESON DESIGN

ART DIRECTOR: STEVE TOLLESON

DESIGNERS: STEVE TOLLESON, MARK WINN

COUNTRY: USA

Client: JUST YOUR TYPE, INC.
Design Firm: GLENN MARTINEZ AND ASSOC.
Art Director/Designer: GLENN MARTINEZ
Country: USA

C L I E N T : R E P R O - P O I N T

D E S I G N F I R M : G R A P H I C - D E S I G N , W E R B E B Ü R O C R E M E R

D E S I G N E R : M A R K U S C R E M E R

I L L U S T R A T O R : A L B E R T M A I E R

C O U N T R Y : G E R M A N Y

CHARGO
PRINTING, INC.
95 Empire Drive
St. Paul, MN 55103
Fax 612/227-2112
Tel 612/227-3003

CHARGO
PRINTING, INC.
95 Empire Drive
St. Paul, MN 55103
Fax 612/227-2112
Tel 612/227-3003

CHARGO
PRINTING, INC.
95 Empire Drive
St. Paul, MN 55103
Fax 612/227-2112
Tel 612/227-3003

Scott T. Lidberg

Client: CHARGO PRINTING, INC.
Design Firm: GRANDPRÉ AND WHALEY, LTD.
Art Director/Designer: KEVIN WHALEY
Country: USA

CLIENT: REX THREE, INC.
DESIGN FIRM: PINKHAUS DESIGN CORP.
ART DIRECTORS: LISA ASHWORTH, JOEL FULLER
DESIGNER: LISA ASHWORTH
ARTIST: RALF SCHUETZ
COUNTRY: USA

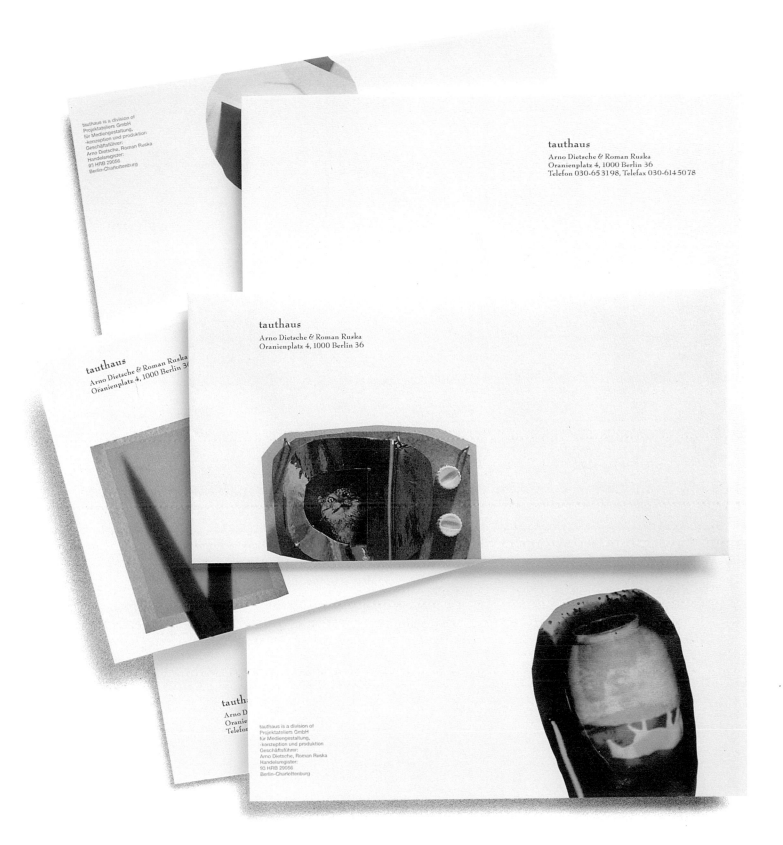

CLIENT: TAUTHAUS
DESIGN FIRM: PROJEKTATELIERS GMBH
ART DIRECTORS: ARNO DIETSCHE, ROMAN RUSKA
DESIGNER: ROMAN RUSKA
PHOTOGRAPHER: ARNO DIETSCHE
COUNTRY: GERMANY

CLIENT: JOANNE DAY
DESIGN FIRM: SMITH GROUP COMMUNICATIONS
DESIGNER: THOM SMITH
COUNTRY: USA

FINELY TUNED
MIKE JOHNSON

FINELY TUNED
MIKE JOHNSON
176 WEST MAIN ST
AVON CT 06001

FINELY TUNED
MIKE JOHNSON
176 WEST MAIN ST
AVON CT 06001
203.677.5766
203.496.1883

176 WEST MAIN ST
AVON CT 06001
203.677.5766
203.496.1883

CLIENT: MIKE JOHNSON
DESIGN FIRM: KEILER DESIGN GROUP
DESIGNER: ELIZABETH DZIERSK
COUNTRY: USA

CLIENT: FOUR GRAPHIC

DESIGN FIRM: COMUNICARTE

ART DIRECTOR: PALO DIAZ

DESIGNERS: PALO DIAZ, PEP CARRIO

COUNTRY: SPAIN

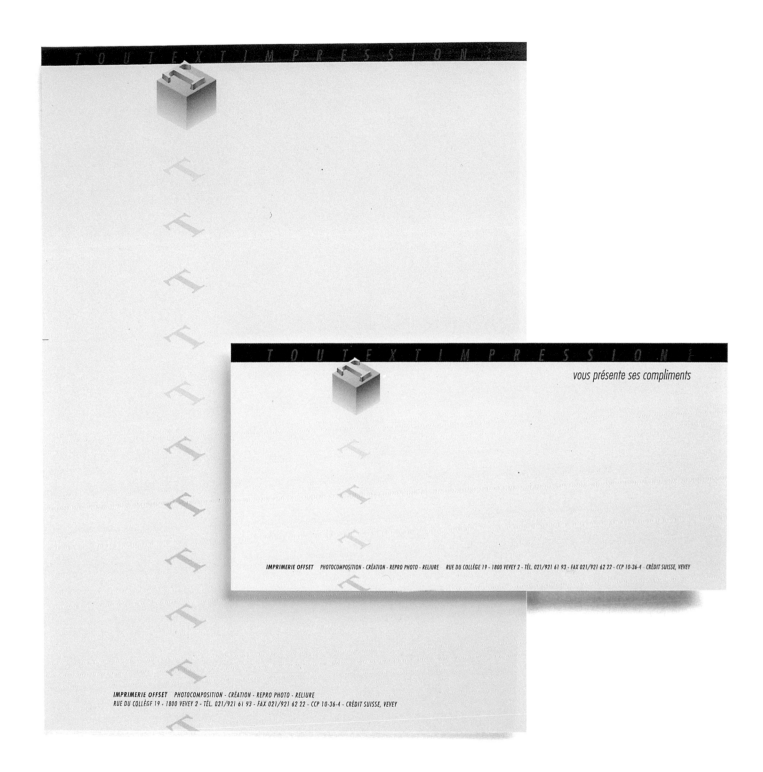

CLIENT: TOUTEXTIMPRESSION
DESIGN FIRM: MAURER INFOGRAPHIE
ART DIRECTOR/DESIGNER: GILBERT MAURER
COUNTRY: SWITZERLAND

CLIENT: BRIAN MEREDITH

DESIGN FIRM: MIRES DESIGN, INC.

ART DIRECTOR/DESIGNER: SCOTT MIRES

ILLUSTRATOR: SEYMOUR CHWAST

COUNTRY: USA

Client: JOAN OSTRIN
Design Firm: SUE CROLICK ADVERTISING + DESIGN
Art Director/Designer: SUE CROLICK
Typographer: GREAT FACES
Country: USA

CLIENT: WRITERS AT WORK
DESIGN FIRM: CLARKSON CREATIVE
ART DIRECTOR/DESIGNER: LARRY CLARKSON
COUNTRY: USA

CLIENT: PETRA GRIEBEL

DESIGN FIRM: CHRISTOF WERTHEFRONGEL

ART DIRECTOR/DESIGNER: CHRISTOF WERTHEFRONGEL

COUNTRY: GERMANY

CLIENT: YVONNE ARMBRUSTER
DESIGNER: JOCHEN GEWECKE
COPYWRITERS: JOCHEN GEWECKE, DOUGLAS ADAMS
COUNTRY: GERMANY

CLIENT: MARLENE MARKS + ASSOCIATES
DESIGN FIRM: MARK OLDACH DESIGN
ART DIRECTOR: MARK OLDACH
DESIGNER: MARK MEYER
COUNTRY: USA

HIRASUNA EDITORIAL

HIRASUNA EDITORIAL

DELPHINE HIRASUNA

901 BATTERY STREET
SUITE 212
SAN FRANCISCO, CA 94111
TEL. 415.986.8014
FAX. 415.986.7649

901 BATTERY STREET
SUITE 212
SAN FRANCISCO, CA 94111
TEL. 415.986.8014
FAX. 415.986.7649

CLIENT: HIRASUNA EDITORIAL
DESIGN FIRM: PENTAGRAM DESIGN
ART DIRECTOR: KIT HINRICHS
DESIGNERS: KIT HINRICHS, CATHERINE WONG
COUNTRY: USA

Buchman Ink, inc.
28906 North Wade Avenue
Wauconda, Illinois 60084
708.526.6149 Phone
708.526.6150 Fax

Buchman Ink, inc.
28906 North Wade Avenue
Wauconda, Illinois 60084
708.526.6149 Phone
708.526.6150 Fax

Aaron Buchman
President

CLIENT: BUCHMAN INK, INC.
DESIGN FIRM: KYM ABRAMS DESIGN, INC.
ART DIRECTOR: KYM ABRAMS
DESIGNER: CHARLYNE FABI
COUNTRY: USA

CLIENT: HELEN BATTERSBY
DESIGN FIRM: HAMBLY & WOOLLEY INC.
ART DIRECTORS: BARBARA WOOLLEY, BOB HAMBLY
DESIGNERS: BOB HAMBLY, BARBARA WOOLLEY
ILLUSTRATOR: BARRY BLITT
COUNTRY: CANADA

Konzepte, Texte, ..., ...
....! ....-
... .: " ....
....? ...., ...
....? " ....,
.... - ....,
... . (...... ....) ....-
...., ...
.... * ....: Ueli Merz,
Apollostrasse 3, CH-8032 Zürich, Tel. 01 382 34 04,
Fax 01 382 29 60.

Konzepte, Texte, ..., ...
....! ....-
... .: " ....
....? ...., ...
....? " ....,
.... - ....,
... . (...... ....) ....-
...., ...
..........., * ....: Ueli Merz,
Apollostrasse 3, CH-8032 Zürich, Tel. 01 382 34 04,
Fax 01 382 29 60.

CLIENT: UELI MERZ

ART DIRECTOR/DESIGNER: HP. SCHNEIDER

COUNTRY: SWITZERLAND

Client: AD WORKS, LTD.

Design Firm: O'KEEFE MARKETING

Art Director: KELLY O'KEEFE

Designer: DAVID KING

Illustrator: JACK WILLIAMS

Country: USA

Linda Chryle writes.

Linda Chryle lives.
843 West Van Buren
No. 211
Chicago, Illinois
60607

Linda Chryle talks.
312.733.1124

And she faxes, too.
312.733.1125

Linda Chryle writes.

843 West Van Buren
No. 211
Chicago, Illinois
60607

Linda Chryle writes.

Linda Chryle lives.
843 West Van Buren
No. 211
Chicago, Illinois
60607

Linda Chryle talks.
312.733.1124

And she faxes, too.
312.733.1125

CLIENT: LINDA CHRYLE

DESIGN FIRM: MARK OLDACH DESIGN

ART DIRECTOR/DESIGNER: MARK OLDACH

COUNTRY: USA

CLIENT: CHUCK CARLSON
DESIGN FIRM: DESIGN METRO
ART DIRECTOR/DESIGNER: SARA ROGERS
COUNTRY: USA

CULINARY · HOTEL

KULINARISCH · HOTEL

RESTAURATION · HÔTELLERIE

CLIENT: PEGGY GREEN
DESIGN FIRM: PENNEBAKER DESIGN
ART DIRECTOR/DESIGNER: JEFFREY McKAY
COUNTRY: USA

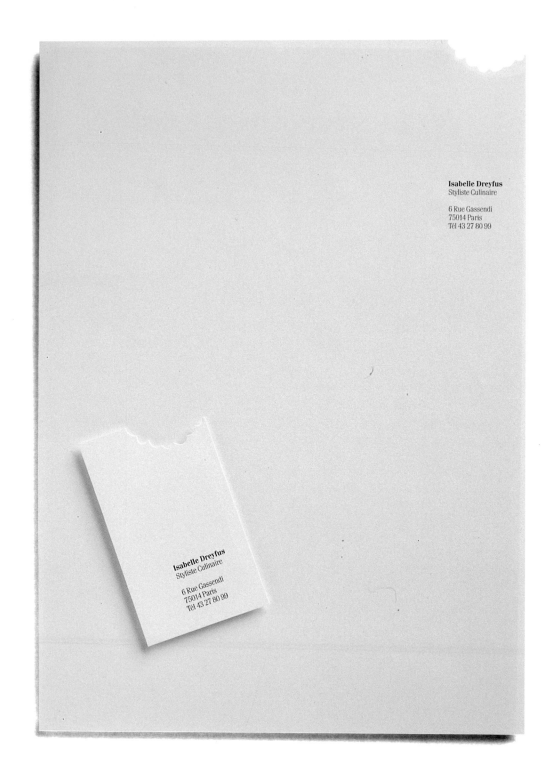

Client: ISABELLE DREYFUS

Design Firm: TOTAL DESIGN SOLOUTION

Art Director/Designer: PAUL VICKERS

Illustrator: PAUL VICKERS

Country: FRANCE

SCHLEIN-DEVEREUX
Catering & Special Events

SCHLEIN-DEVEREUX
Catering & Special Events

1141 East 11th Street
Houston, Texas 77009

1141 East 11th Street
Houston, Texas 77009
713.861.6769

Client: SCHLEIN-DEVEREUX
Design Firm: HILL/A MARKETING DESIGN GROUP
Art Director: CHRIS HILL
Designers: CHRIS HILL, CHUCK THURMAN
Photographer: GARY FAYE
Country: USA

Oakland

Oakland Fast Food

Telford Place,
Crawley,
West Sussex,
RH10 1SY.

Telephone:
0293-33222.
Fax:
0293-24705.

A Division of
Grand Metropolitan
Foods Europe Ltd.
Registered Office:
430 Victoria Road,
South Ruislip,
Middlesex.
Registered Number:
207795.

Oakland
David Dawson   Tel: 0293-33222.
Financial Controller   Fax: 0293-24705.

Oakland Fast Food,
Telford Place,
Crawley,
West Sussex,
RH10 1SY.

CLIENT: OAKLAND FAST FOOD
DESIGN FIRM: ROUNDEL DESIGN GROUP
ART DIRECTOR: MICHAEL DENNY
DESIGNER: JOHN BATESON
COUNTRY: GREAT BRITAIN

CLIENT: ONE FIFTH AVENUE
DESIGN FIRM: PENTAGRAM
ART DIRECTOR: PAULA SCHER
DESIGNERS: PAULA SCHER, RON LOUIE
COUNTRY: USA

Client: MENU DOS
Design Firm: S.G. STUDIO
Art Director/Designer: VICKY METZGER
Illustrator: VICKY METZGER
Copywriter: JOSÉ METZGER
Country: SPAIN

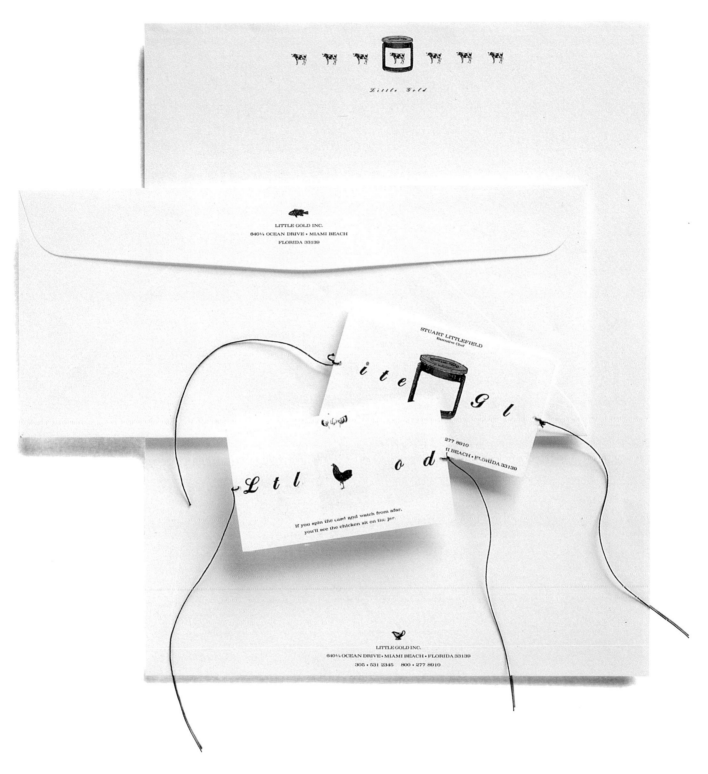

CLIENT: TONY GOLDMAN
DESIGN FIRM: SAGMEISTER GRAPHICS
ART DIRECTOR/DESIGNER: STEFAN SAGMEISTER
ILLUSTRATOR: STEFAN SAGMEISTER
COUNTRY: USA

SEE ME · EAT ME

PUFF FAIRCLOUGH · FOOD
5A BURLINGTON LODGE
BUER ROAD, LONDON
TELEPHONE 01 736

SEE ME · EAT ME

PUFF FAIRCLOUGH · FOOD STYLIST
5A BURLINGTON LODGE STUDIO
BUER ROAD, LONDON SW6 4LA
TELEPHONE 01 736 0623

CLIENT: PUFF FAIRCLOUGH
DESIGN FIRM: LEWIS MOBERLY
ART DIRECTOR: MARY LEWIS
DESIGNER: KARIN DUNBAR
PHOTOGRAPHER: LAURIE EVANS
COUNTRY: GREAT BRITAIN

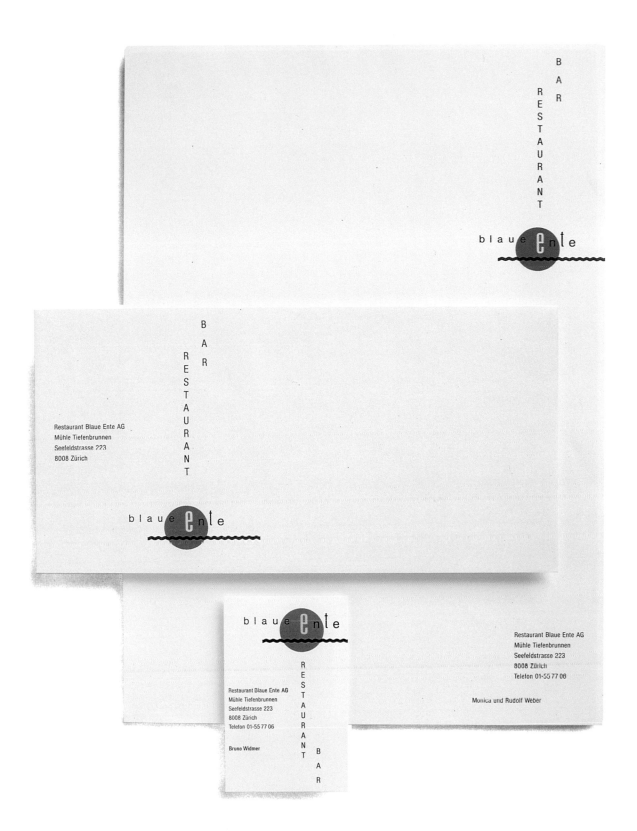

CLIENT: RESTAURANT BLAUE ENTE
DESIGN FIRM: WEIERSMÜLLER BOSSHARD GRÜNINGER
DESIGNERS: R. WEIERSMÜLLER, M. BOSSHARD
COUNTRY: SWITZERLAND

Client: ANGEL FOOD
Design Firm: MARIS, WEST & BAKER, INC.
Art Director/Designer: BILL PORCH
Illustrator: BILL PORCH
Country: USA

CLIENT: MOOSE'S
DESIGN FIRM: SCHUMAKER
DESIGNER: WARD SCHUMAKER
ILLUSTRATOR: WARD SCHUMAKER
COUNTRY: USA

CLIENT: THE COPLEY SQUARE HOTEL
DESIGN FIRM: MIDNIGHT OIL STUDIOS
ART DIRECTOR: JAMES M. SKILES
DESIGNER: KATHRYN A. KLEIN
ILLUSTRATOR: KATHRYN A. KLEIN
COUNTRY: USA

DESIGNERS

DESIGNERS

DESIGNERS

CLIENT: UGO VALESIO

DESIGNER: UGO VALESIO

COUNTRY: ITALY

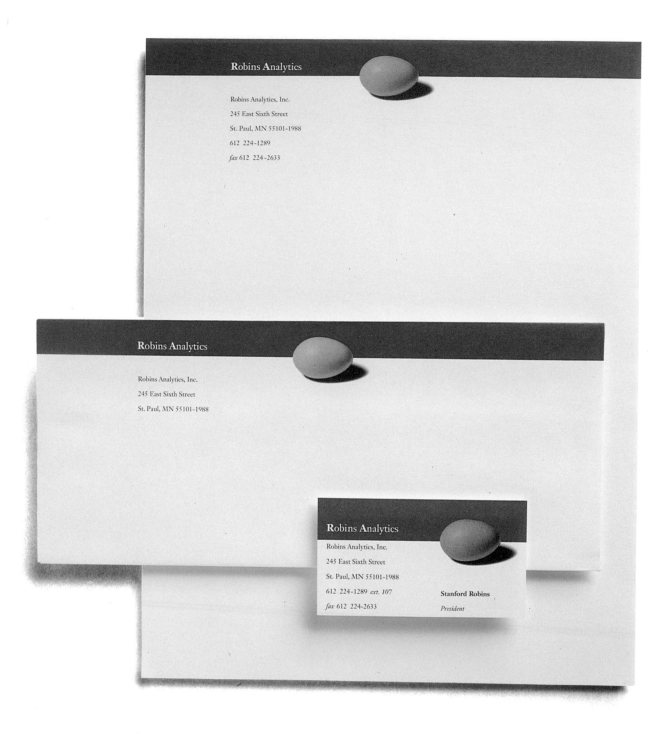

CLIENT: ROBINS ANALYTICS, INC.
ART DIRECTOR/DESIGNER: JANE TILKA
PHOTOGRAPHER: JOE MICHL
COUNTRY: USA

Client: PETER FISHEL
Design Firm: FISHEL DESIGN
Designer: PETER FISHEL
Country: USA

HBK WAGNER · ROSENSTRASSE 15 · 2870 DELMENHORST
TELEFON 0 42 21 - 15 00 12 · TELEFAX 0 42 21 - 15 00 16

HORST SEIDLER · · INHABER HANS WAGNER · BRANDTSTRASSE 22 · D-2800 BREMEN 1 · TELEFON 04 21 - 37 17 07
BANK: BREMER LANDESBANK · BLZ 290 500 00 · KTO.-NR. 1003845005 · EINGETRAGEN AMTSGERICHT BREMEN HRA 13092
POST: HBK WAGNER DESIGN · ROSENSTRASSE 15 · D-2870 DELMENHORST · TELEFON 0 42 21 - 15 00 12 · FAX 0 42 21 - 15 00 16

CLIENT: WAGNER DESIGN
DESIGN FIRM: ATELIER HAASE & KNELS
ART DIRECTOR/DESIGNER: SIBYLLE HAASE
COUNTRY: GERMANY

CLIENT: CRAIG CUTLER STUDIO, INC.
DESIGN FIRM: THE PUSHPIN GROUP
ART DIRECTOR/DESIGNER: GREG SIMPSON
COUNTRY: USA

Client: ENVIROGRAPHICS
Design Firm: PETER GOOD GRAPHIC DESIGN
Art Director/Designer: PETER GOOD
Illustrator: EDWARD KIM
Country: USA

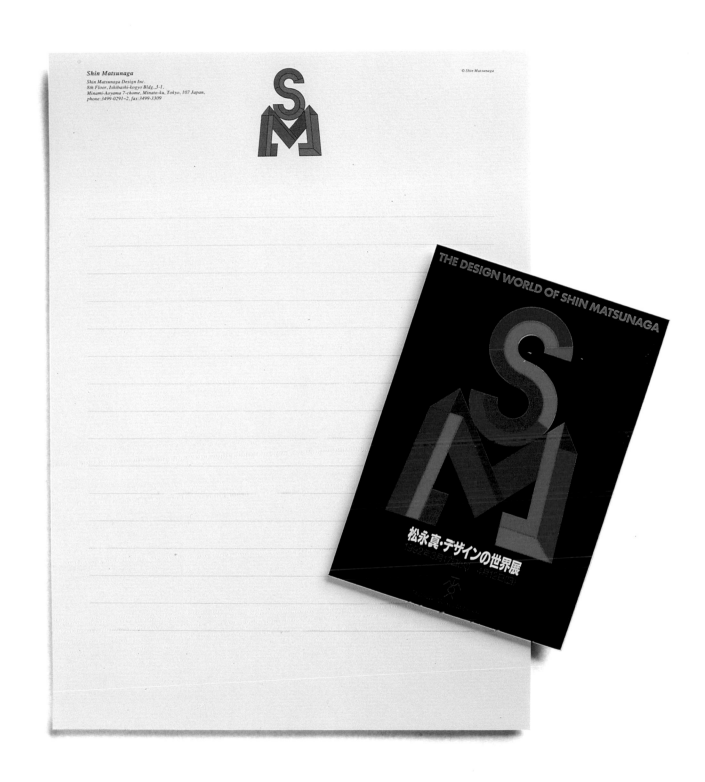

Shin Matsunaga
Shin Matsunaga Design Inc.
8th Floor, Ishibashi-kogyo Bldg. 3-1,
Minami-Aoyama 7-chome, Minato-ku, Tokyo, 107 Japan,
phone:3499-0291~2, fax:3499-3309

© Shin Matsunaga

THE DESIGN WORLD OF SHIN MATSUNAGA

松永真・デザインの世界展

CLIENT: SHIN MATSUNAGA DESIGN INC.

ART DIRECTOR/DESIGNER: SHIN MATSUNAGA

COUNTRY: JAPAN

CLIENT: PEN PLUS INCORPORATED

DESIGN FIRM: M PLUS M INCORPORATED

ART DIRECTORS: TAKAAKI MATSUMOTO, MICHAEL McGINN

DESIGNER: TAKAAKI MATSUMOTO

COUNTRY: USA

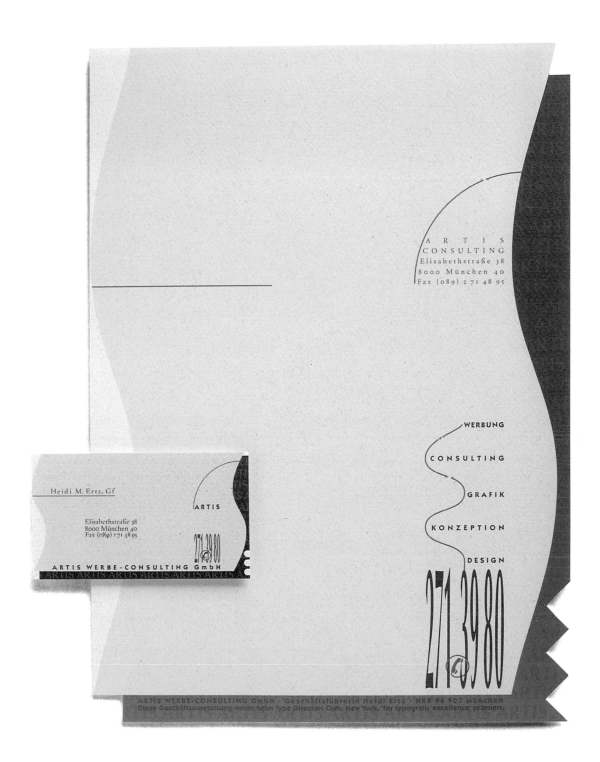

CLIENT: ARTIS WERBE-CONSULTING

DESIGN FIRM: ARTIS WERBE-CONSULTING

ART DIRECTOR/DESIGNER: MICHAEL MOESSLANG

COUNTRY: GERMANY

CLIENT: DESIGN DEPT.
DESIGN FIRM: DESIGN DEPT.
ART DIRECTORS: JÉROME OUDIN, JÉROME SAINT-LOUBERT BLÉ, SUSANNA SHANNON
DESIGNERS: JÉROME OUDIN, JÉROME SAINT-LOUBERT BLÉ, SUSANNA SHANNON
COUNTRY: FRANCE

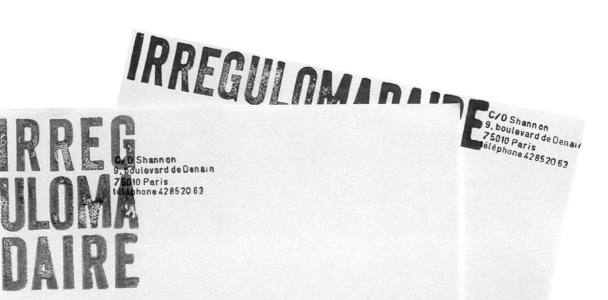

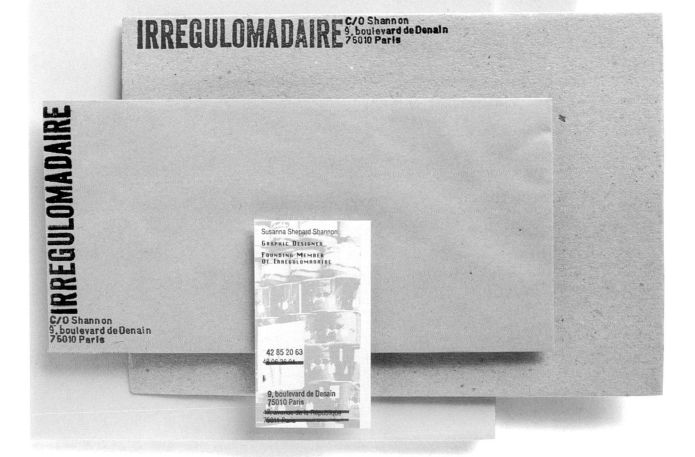

CLIENT: IRREGULOMADAIRE

DESIGN FIRM: DESIGN DEPT.

ART DIRECTORS: JÉROME OUDIN, JÉROME SAINT-LOUBERT BLÉ, SUSANNA SHANNON

DESIGNERS: JÉROME OUDIN, JÉROME SAINT-LOUBERT BLÉ, SUSANNA SHANNON

COUNTRY: FRANCE

Client: BRIGHT IDEAS
Design Firm: KYM ABRAMS DESIGN
Art Director/Designer: KYM ABRAMS
Country: USA

CLIENT: MULLER + COMPANY
DESIGN FIRM: MULLER + COMPANY
ART DIRECTOR/DESIGNER: JOHN MULLER
COUNTRY: USA

Client: WET PAPER BAG
Design Firm: WET PAPER BAG GRAPHIC DESIGN
Art Director/Designer: LEWIS GLASER
Calligrapher: LEWIS GLASER
Country: USA

The
Weller
Institute
For
The
Cure
Of
Design,
Inc.

3091
Fawn
Drive
P O Box
726
Park
City,
Utah
84060

Please
Call
(801)
649-9859
And
Or
Fax
(801)
649-4196

Home
Office,
Studio
And
Head
quarters:
Cutting
Horse
Division

CLIENT: THE WELLER INSTITUTE FOR THE CURE OF DESIGN

DESIGN FIRM: THE WELLER INSTITUTE FOR THE CURE OF DESIGN

ART DIRECTOR/DESIGNER: DON WELLER

COUNTRY: USA

A MARKETING DESIGN GROUP

A MARKETING DESIGN GROUP   CHRIS HILL

3512 LAKE STREET
HOUSTON, TEXAS 77098
713.523.7363
FAX 713.523.6624

A MARKETING DESIGN GROUP

3512 LAKE STREET   HOUSTON, TEXAS 77098.5518   713.523.7363   FAX 713.523.6624

CLIENT: HILL/A MARKETING DESIGN GROUP
DESIGN FIRM: HILL/A MARKETING DESIGN GROUP
ART DIRECTOR: CHRIS HILL
DESIGNERS: CHRIS HILL, JOE RATTAN
COUNTRY: USA

CLIENT: DEAN GERRIE DESIGN
ART DIRECTOR: DEAN GERRIE
DESIGNER: MARIE WIRTZ
COUNTRY: USA

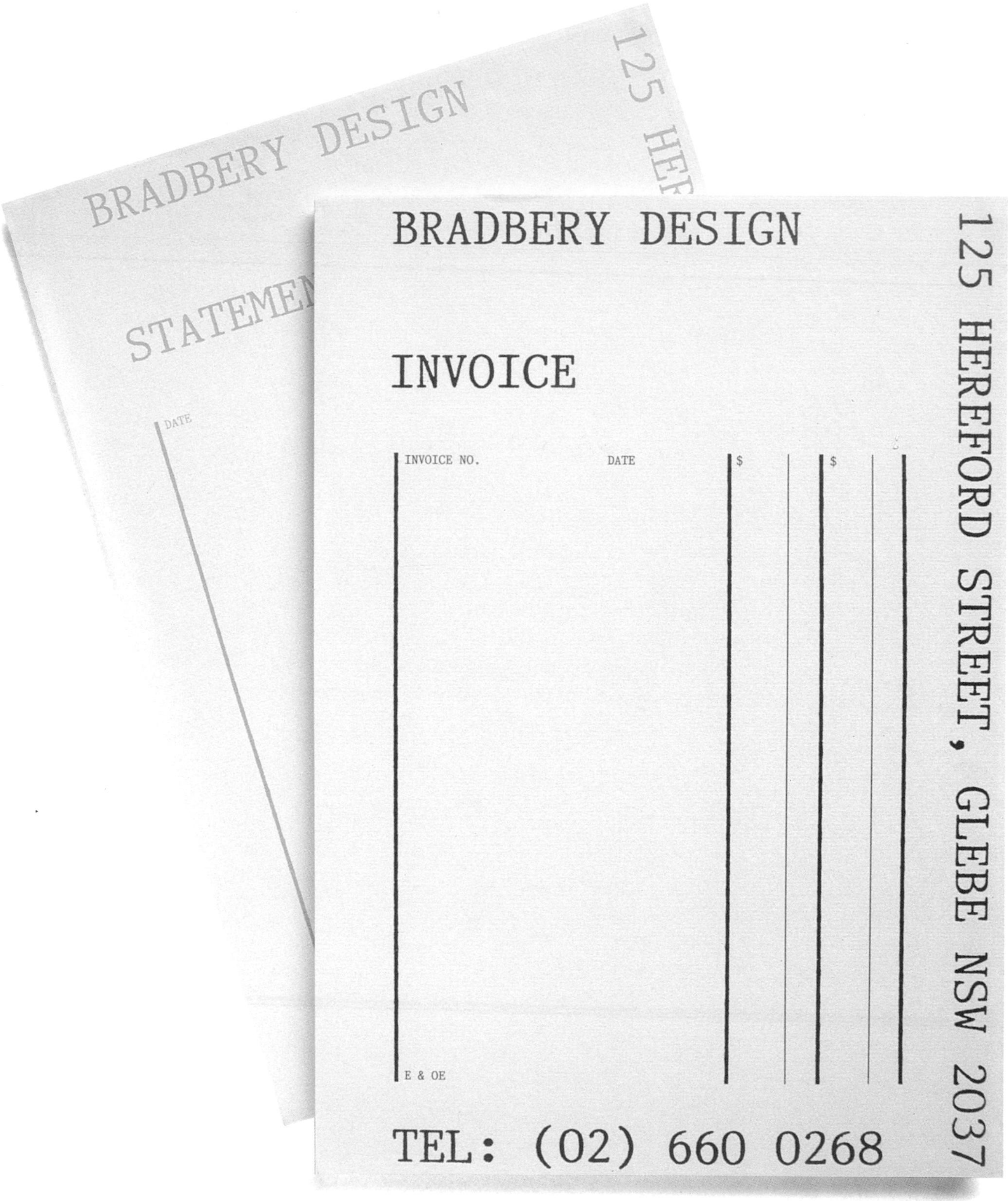
BRADBERY DESIGN
STATEMEN
DATE
125 HER
BRADBERY DESIGN
INVOICE
INVOICE NO.
DATE
$
$
E & OE
TEL: (02) 660 0268
125 HEREFORD STREET, GLEBE NSW 2037

CLIENT: BRADBERY DESIGN
ART DIRECTOR/DESIGNER: IAN BRADBERY
COUNTRY: AUSTRALIA

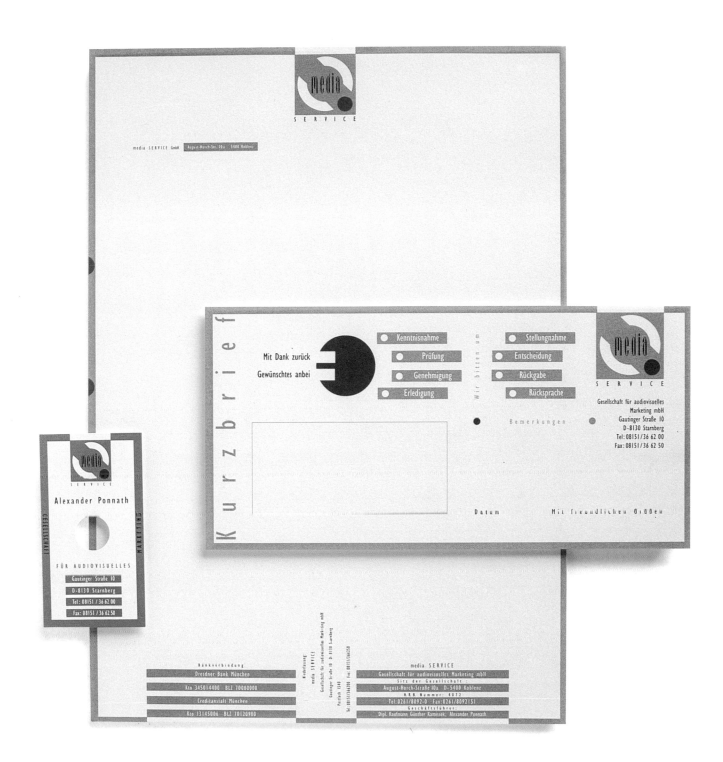

Client: MEDIA SERVICE
Design Firm: KREATIV PAWLITZEK + KRUEGER
Art Director: KONSTANTIN KRUEGER
Designer: MARTINA MÜLLER
Country: GERMANY

MARION

Marion Graphics
3701 W. Alabama, Suite 380
Houston, Texas 77027
(713) 623-6444

MARION

Marion Graphics
3701 W. Alabama, Suite 380
Houston, Texas 77027

MARION

Marion Graphics
3701 W. Alabama, Suite 380
Houston, Texas 77027
Charles Freeman   (713) 623-6444

CLIENT: MARION GRAPHICS
DESIGN FIRM: CHARLES FREEMAN
ART DIRECTOR/DESIGNER: CHARLES FREEMAN
COUNTRY: USA

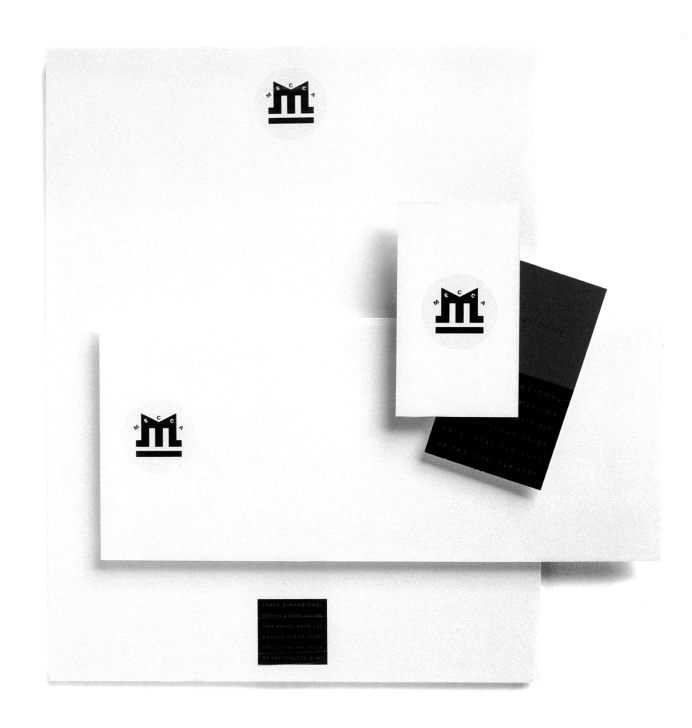

CLIENT: GEORGE MECCA

ART DIRECTOR/DESIGNER: THOMAS VASQUEZ

ILLUSTRATOR: THOMAS VASQUEZ

COUNTRY: USA

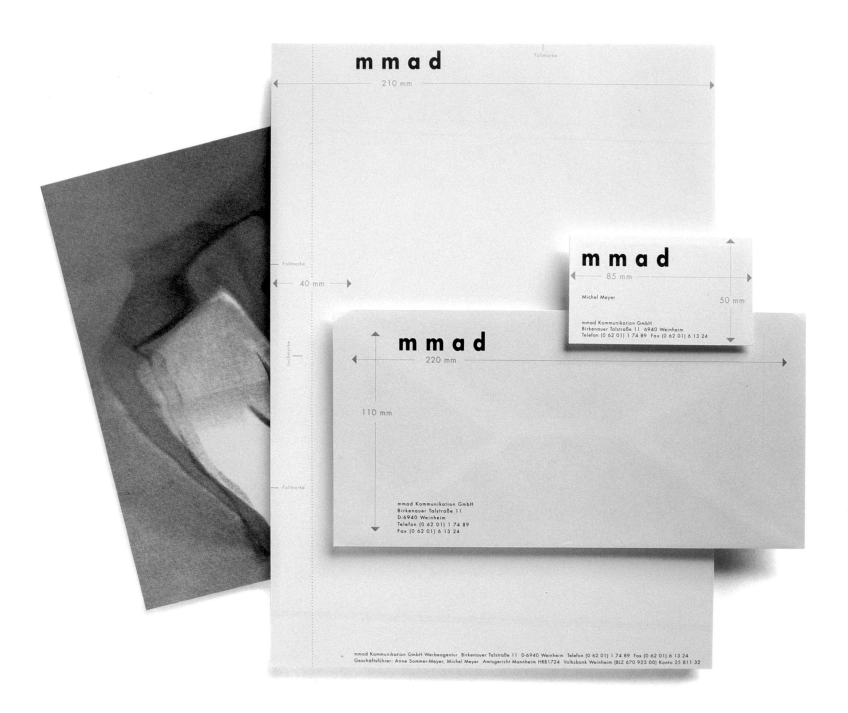

CLIENT: MMAD KOMMUNIKATION
DESIGN FIRM: MMAD
ART DIRECTOR/DESIGNER: ANNE SOMMER-MEYER
COUNTRY: GERMANY

SEAN BUTCHER
DESIGNER

SEAN BUTCHER
DESIGNER

BURLEY GRANGE · MILL LAWN
BURLEY · HANTS · BH24 4HP
TELEPHONE 04253 2209

BURLEY GRANGE · MILL LAWN
BURLEY · HANTS · BH24 4HP
TELEPHONE 04253 2209

CLIENT: SEAN BUTCHER
ART DIRECTOR/DESIGNER: SEAN BUTCHER
COUNTRY: GREAT BRITAIN

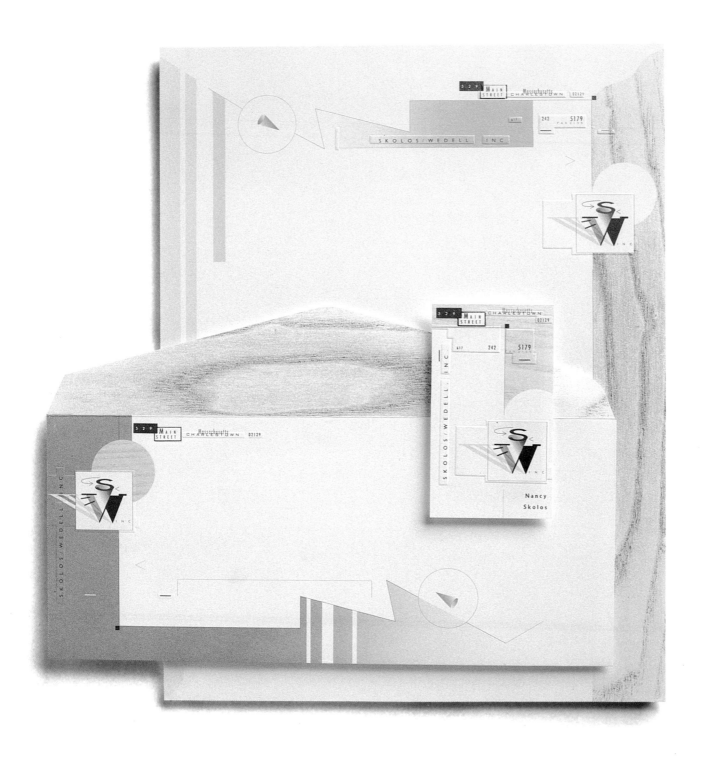

CLIENT: SKOLOS/WEDELL, INC.

DESIGNER: NANCY SKOLOS

COUNTRY: USA

CLIENT: CONCRETE DESIGN COMMUNICATIONS INC.

DESIGN FIRM: CONCRETE DESIGN COMMUNICATIONS INC.

ART DIRECTORS/DESIGNERS: DITI KATONA, JOHN PYLYPCZAK

ILLUSTRATOR: ROSS MACDONALD

COUNTRY: CANADA

CLIENT: MARK WOOD DESIGN OFFICE

DESIGN FIRM: MARK WOOD DESIGN OFFICE

ART DIRECTOR/DESIGNER: MARK WOOD

COUNTRY: USA

CLIENT: TARZAN COMMUNICATION GRAPHIQUE
DESIGN FIRM: TARZAN COMMUNICATION GRAPHIQUE
ART DIRECTOR: TARZAN COMMUNICATION GRAPHIQUE
DESIGNER: TARZAN COMMUNICATION GRAPHIQUE
PHOTOGRAPHER: ADRIAN DUEY
COUNTRY: CANADA

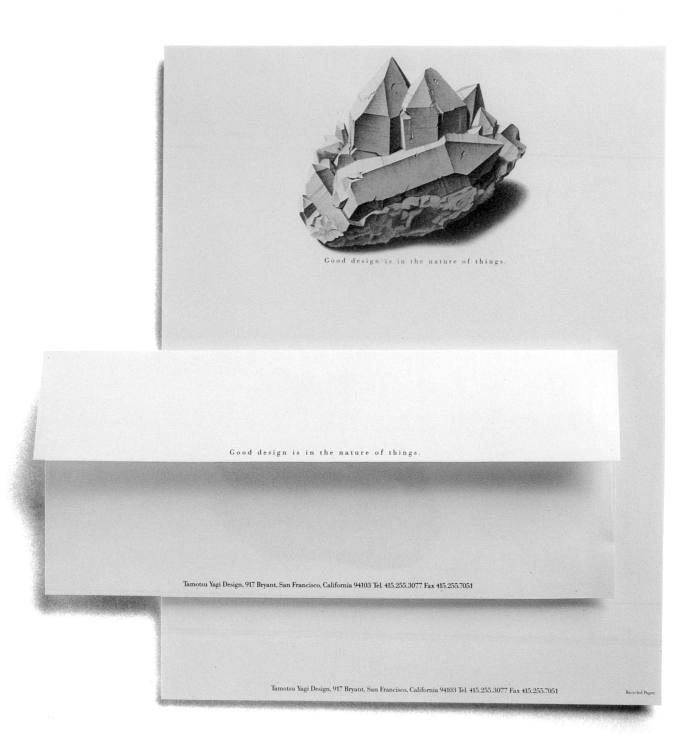

Good design is in the nature of things.

Good design is in the nature of things.

Tamotsu Yagi Design, 917 Bryant, San Francisco, California 94103 Tel. 415.255.3077 Fax 415.255.7051

Tamotsu Yagi Design, 917 Bryant, San Francisco, California 94103 Tel. 415.255.3077 Fax 415.255.7051

Recycled Paper

C LIENT : TAMOTSU YAGI DESIGN
D ESIGN F IRM : TAMOTSU YAGI DESIGN
A RT D IRECTOR : TAMOTSU YAGI
D ESIGNER : DELRAE ROTH
C OUNTRY : USA

George Cheng graphic designer

George Cheng graphic designer

George Cheng graphic designer
20 Demarest Ave. Englewood Cliffs, N.J. 07632   201 816 9362

20 Demarest Avenue Englewood Cliffs, N.J. 07632

CLIENT: GEORGE CHENG
DESIGNER: GEORGE CHENG
COUNTRY: USA

Client: BOB HOWER
Design Firm: DOUBLE VISION
Art Directors/Designers: MARY CAWEIN, WALTER McCORD
Illustrators: MARY CAWEIN, WALTER McCORD
Country: USA

CLIENT: DEARWATER DESIGN
DESIGN FIRM: DEARWATER DESIGN
ART DIRECTOR: ANDY DEARWATER
COUNTRY: USA

EWALD WOLF
•
Eppendorfer Landstr. 24
•
2000 Hamburg 20
•
Telefon 040/46 57 04

EWALD WOLF
Eppendorfer Landstr. 24 • 2000 Hamburg 20 • Telefon 040/46 57 04

CLIENT: EWALD WOLF
DESIGN FIRM: SCHOLZ AND FRIENDS
ART DIRECTOR: CARSTEN BUCK
ILLUSTRATOR: GERD WERNER
COUNTRY: GERMANY

CLIENT: TODD HAUSWIRTH DESIGN
DESIGN FIRM: CHARLES S. ANDERSON DESIGN
ART DIRECTOR/DESIGNER: TODD HAUSWIRTH
ILLUSTRATOR: TODD HAUSWIRTH
COUNTRY: USA

CLIENT: WHITE DESIGN
DESIGN FIRM: WHITE DESIGN
ART DIRECTOR: JOHN WHITE
DESIGNERS: JOHN WHITE, ARAM YOUSSEFIAN
COUNTRY: USA

FASHION

MODE

MODE

CLIENT: ADVENTURE 16
DESIGN FIRM: MIRES DESIGN, INC.
ART DIRECTOR/DESIGNER: JOSE SERRANO
ILLUSTRATOR: DAN THONER
COUNTRY: USA

Client: ABBY E. HERGET
Design Firm: HERGET DESIGN
Designer: ABBY E. HERGET
Country: USA

CLIENT: RANDY CARRUCCI
DESIGN FIRM: MIRES DESIGN
ART DIRECTOR/DESIGNER: SCOTT MIRES
COUNTRY: USA

CLIENT: AMBATTUR CLOTHING CO.
DESIGN FIRM: ANNETTE HARCUS DESIGN
ART DIRECTOR: ANNETTE HARCUS
DESIGNERS: KRISTEN THIEME, ANNETTE HARCUS
COUNTRY: AUSTRALIA

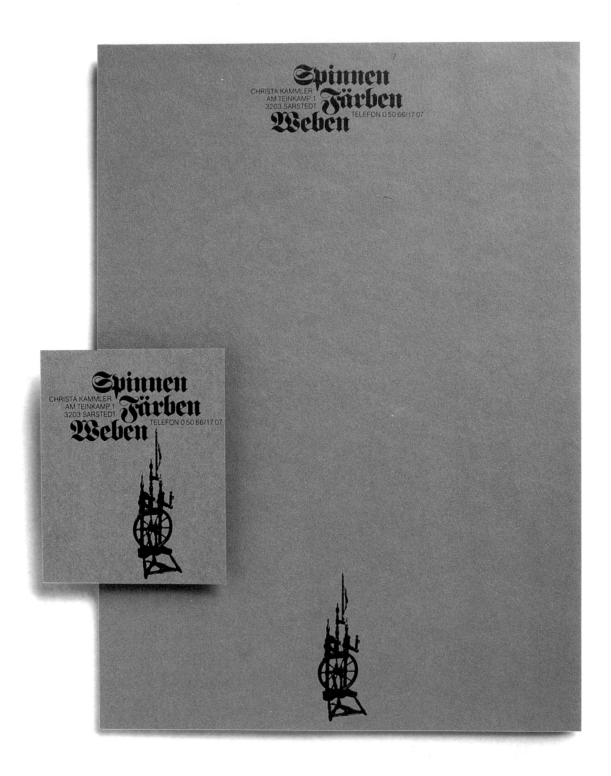

Client: CHRISTA KAMMLER

Design Firm: SIEGFRIED WERBUNG

Art Director/Designer: PETER SIEGFRIED

Country: GERMANY

Client: H₂O PLUS
Design Firm: MURRIE LIENHART RYSNER & ASSOCIATES
Art Director/Designer: JIM LIENHART
Country: USA

CLIENT: GA-GA-GOO!
DESIGN FIRM: TIMEBOMB
DESIGNER: ANTHONY MARSHALL
COUNTRY: USA

Nathalie Dufour-Samson

ADRESSE POSTALE   DIRECTRICE   SIÈGE DE L'ASSOCIATION

12, RUE RENAULT, 94160 SAINT-MANDÉ   107, RUE DE RIVOLI, 75001 PARIS

Association Nationale pour le Développement des Arts de la Mode

TEL 43 65 29 87 FAX 43 65 46 86   TEL 40 15 74 71 FAX 40 15 74 14

CLIENT: ANDAM
DESIGN FIRM: BELL & CO.
ART DIRECTOR/DESIGNER: GARTH BELL
ILLUSTRATOR: GARTH BELL
COUNTRY: FRANCE

CLIENT: KAY LAWRENCE
DESIGN FIRM: JOHN NOWLAND DESIGN
ART DIRECTOR: JOHN NOWLAND
DESIGNERS: JOHN NOWLAND, CHRISTOPHER BALL
COUNTRY: AUSTRALIA

INDUSTRY

INDUSTRIE

INDUSTRIE

Client: DELEO CLAY TILE

Design Firm: MIRES DESIGN, INC.

Art Director/Designer: SCOTT MIRES

Country: USA

CLIENT: BERGMANN WASMER & ASSOCIATES, INC.

ART DIRECTOR/DESIGNER: DAVID WARREN

ILLUSTRATOR: DIEGO RUIZ

COUNTRY: USA

WALLACE JAMES SHAW
56 PELHAM LANE
WILTON, CONNECTICUT 06897
TEL (203) 761-1176
NY TEL (914) 632-1774

WALLACE JAMES SHAW
56 PELHAM LANE
WILTON, CONNECTICUT 06897
TEL (203) 761-1176
NY TEL (914) 632-1774

WALLACE JAMES SHAW
56 PELHAM LANE
WILTON, CONNECTICUT 06897

CLIENT: SHAW NAUTICAL
DESIGN FIRM: WALLACE CHURCH ASSOCIATES, INC.
ART DIRECTORS: STANLEY CHURCH, ROBERT WALLACE
DESIGNER/ILLUSTRATOR: JOE CUTICONE
COUNTRY: USA

Hillcrest Construction, Inc.
3402 McFarlin Suite 210
Dallas, Texas 75205
214-522-5094
Fax 214-522-5095

CLIENT: HILLCREST CONSTRUCTION, INC.

DESIGN FIRM: EISENBERG AND ASSOCIATES

ART DIRECTORS: TIFFANY TAYLOR, ARTHUR EISENBERG

DESIGNER: TIFFANY TAYLOR

COUNTRY: USA

CLIENT: GLASSWORKS
DESIGN FIRM: HORNALL ANDERSON DESIGN WORKS
ART DIRECTOR: JACK ANDERSON
DESIGNERS: JACK ANDERSON, DAVID BATES
COUNTRY: USA

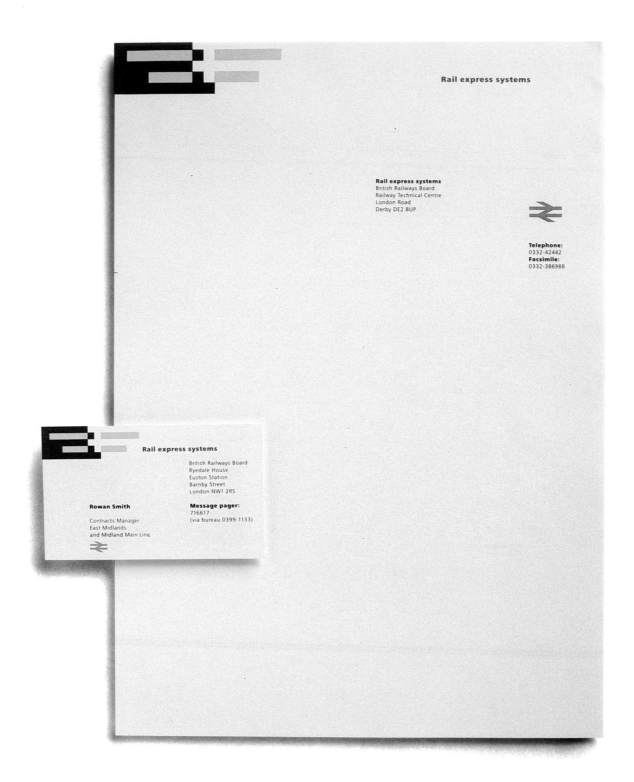

CLIENT: RAIL EXPRESS SYSTEMS

DESIGN FIRM: ROUNDEL DESIGN GROUP

ART DIRECTOR: MICHAEL DENNY

DESIGNERS: JOHN BATESON, HAROLD BATTEN, DARREN RICHARDSON

COUNTRY: GREAT BRITAIN

CLIENT: IBM LATIN AMERICA
DESIGN FIRM: LOPEZ SALPETER & ASSOC.
ART DIRECTOR/DESIGNER: BOB SALPETER
ILLUSTRATOR: ALEX TIANI
COUNTRY: USA

Client: OUTERSPACE
Design Firm: SARGENT & BERMAN
Art Directors: PETER SARGENT, GREG BERMAN
Designer: KRISTIN LOTZ
Country: USA

BRICK CHAPMAN
VICE PRESIDENT
FACILITIES

PACIFIC DESIGN CENTER
8687 MELROSE AVENUE
LOS ANGELES CA, 90069
TEL: 310.657.0800
FAX: 310.652.8576

MICHELLE HARRINGTON
CONTROLLER

PACIFIC DESIGN CENTER
8687 MELROSE AVENUE
LOS ANGELES, CA 90069
TEL: 310. 657. 0800
FAX: 310. 652. 8576

PACIFIC DESIGN CENTER
8687 MELROSE AVENUE
LOS ANGELES
CALIFORNIA 90069

CLIENT: PACIFIC DESIGN CENTER
DESIGN FIRM: PENTAGRAM DESIGN
ART DIRECTOR: KIT HINRICHS
DESIGNER: MARK T. SELFE
COUNTRY: USA

CLIENT: SABINE MOSKAT

DESIGNER: KURT DORNIG

COUNTRY: AUSTRIA

The centre for design
and innovation

Le centre pour
le design et l'innovation

DESIGN EXCHANGE

P.O. Box 18
Toronto-Dominion Centre
Toronto, Canada M5K 1B2
Tel: (416) 363-6121
Fax: (416) 368-0684

DESIGN EXCHANGE

P.O. Box 18
Toronto-Dominion Centre
Toronto, Canada M5K 1B2
Tel: (416) 363-6121
Fax: (416) 368-0684

CLIENT: DESIGN EXCHANGE
DESIGN FIRM: CONCRETE DESIGN COMMUNICATIONS INC.
ART DIRECTORS: DITI KATONA, JOHN PYLYPCZAK
DESIGNER: JOHN PYLYPCZAK
COUNTRY: CANADA

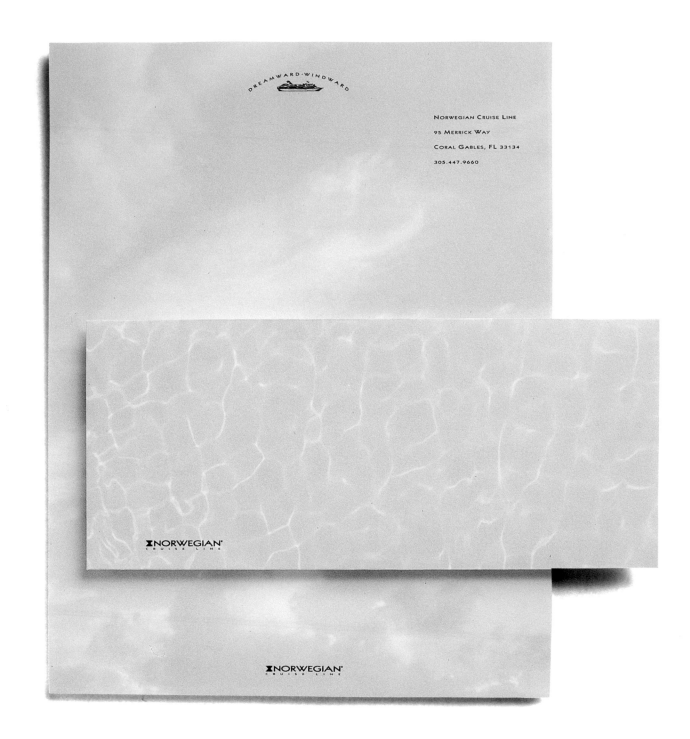

CLIENT: NORWEGIAN CRUISE LINE

AGENCY: GOODBY, BERLIN & SILVERSTEIN

STUDIO: LISA LEVIN DESIGN

ART DIRECTOR/DESIGNER: LISA LEVIN

COUNTRY: USA

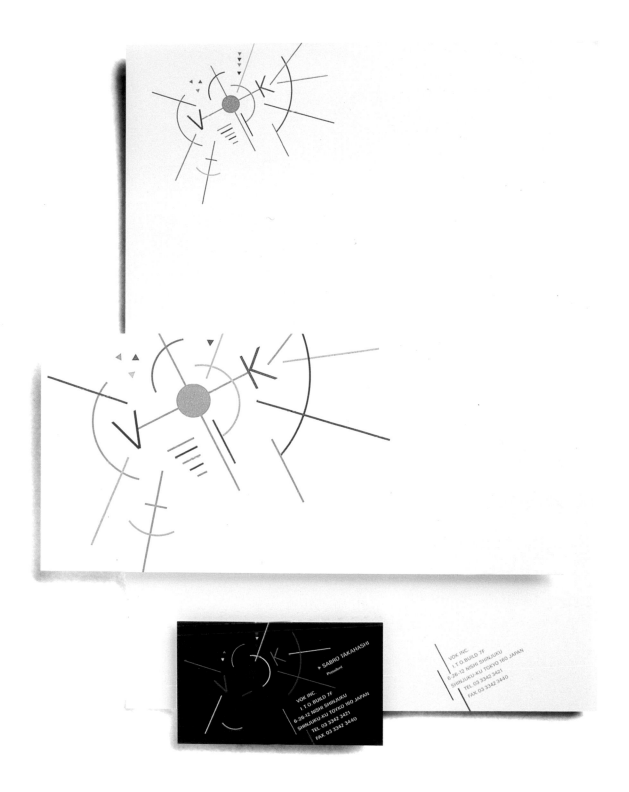

CLIENT: VOK INC.
DESIGN FIRM: INAYOSHI DESIGN INC.
ART DIRECTOR: HIROMI INAYOSHI
DESIGNER: MIHA TAKAGI
COUNTRY: JAPAN

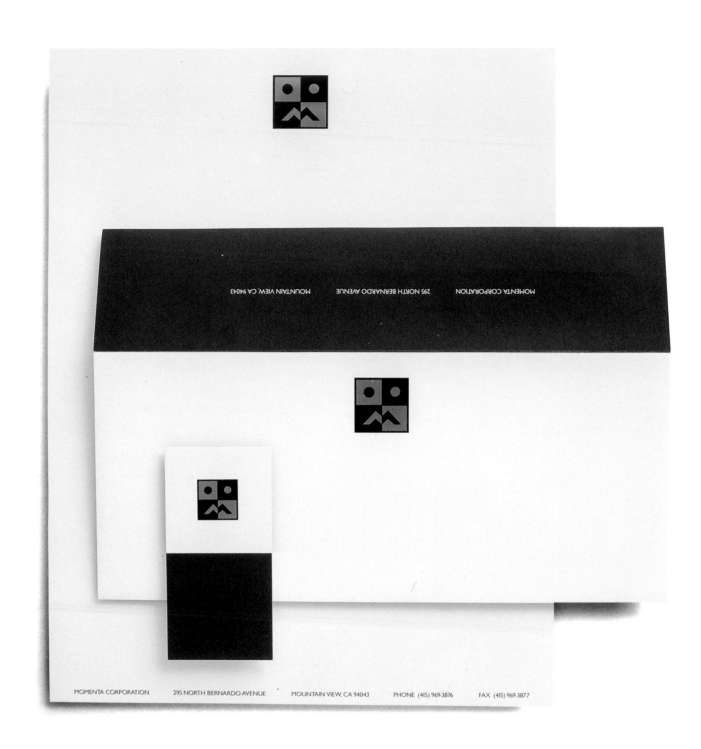

MOMENTA CORPORATION   295 NORTH BERNARDO AVENUE   MOUNTAIN VIEW, CA 94043   PHONE (415) 969-3876   FAX (415) 969-3877

CLIENT: MOMENTA CORPORATION
DESIGN FIRM: ALTMAN & MANLEY
ART DIRECTORS: BRENT CROXTON, PAUL HUBER
DESIGNERS: BRENT CROXTON, ALBERT DOWNS
COUNTRY: USA

CLIENT: HUBERT PATTIEU

ART DIRECTOR/DESIGNER: HUBERT PATTIEU

COUNTRY: FRANCE

CLIENT: FURNITURE FILE
ART DIRECTORS: ADRIAN WHITEFOORD, SIMON PEMBERTON
DESIGNER: LIZ PIPER
COUNTRY: GREAT BRITAIN

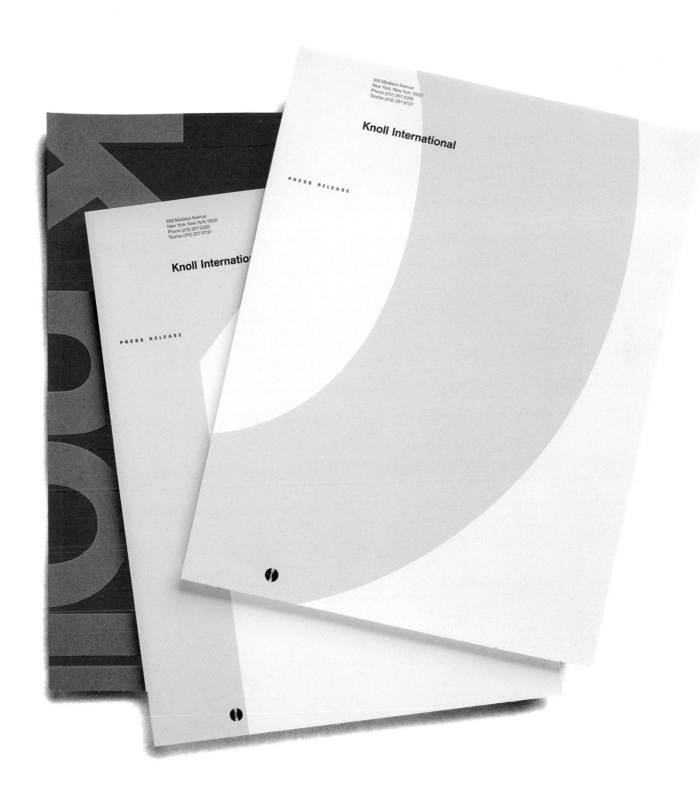

CLIENT: KNOLL INTERNATIONAL
DESIGN FIRM: KNOLL GRAPHICS
ART DIRECTOR: ALISON CHOATE
DESIGNERS: ALISON CHOATE, SUSAN MORIGUCHI, TIBOR KALMAN
COUNTRY: USA

CLIENT: ALINEA AG
DESIGN FIRM: HAS DESIGN
ART DIRECTORS: GARY ALPERN, ANDRES HASLER, THEO SCHNELL
COUNTRY: SWITZERLAND

CLIENT: KEILHAUER INDUSTRIES LTD.
DESIGN FIRM: VANDERBYL DESIGN
ART DIRECTOR/DESIGNER: MICHAEL VANDERBYL
COUNTRY: USA

CLIENT: CHANDLER ATTWOOD LIMITED
DESIGN FIRM: WERNER DESIGN WERKS INC.
ART DIRECTOR/DESIGNER: SHARON WERNER
ILLUSTRATORS: SHARON WERNER, LYNN SCHULTE
COUNTRY: USA

CLIENT: ARCHITECTURAL RESPONSE KOLLECTION, INC.

DESIGN FIRM: LOOKING

ART DIRECTOR/DESIGNER: JOHN CLARK

ILLUSTRATOR: JOHN CLARK

COUNTRY: USA

CLIENT: WINGER MUSCLE THERAPY
DESIGN FIRM: SWIETER DESIGN
ART DIRECTOR: JOHN SWIETER
DESIGNERS: JOHN SWIETER, JIM VOGEL
COUNTRY: USA

CLIENT: DR. CARYN HALPERN
DESIGN FIRM: KNAPE & KNAPE
ART DIRECTOR: WILLIE BARONET
DESIGNER: MICHAEL CONNORS
COUNTRY: USA

LITTLE TOKYO DENTAL GROUP

小東京歯科医院

IWAO YOSHIMURA, D.D.S.

HIROTO KANAI, D.D.S.

SUSAN TAKEI, D.D.S.

316 E. Second Street

Suite 301

Los Angeles

CA 90012

213/680-9935

SUSAN TAKEI, D.D.S.

歯科医　武井　悦子

LITTLE TOKYO DENTAL GROUP

小東京歯科医院

316 E. Second Street, Suite 301

Los Angeles, CA 90012

213/680-9935

316 E. Second Street

Suite 301

Los Angeles, CA 90012

小東京歯科医院

LITTLE TOKYO DENTAL GROUP

Client: LITTLE TOKYO DENTAL GROUP
Design Firm: VERA DESIGN
Designer: JOE VERA
Country: USA

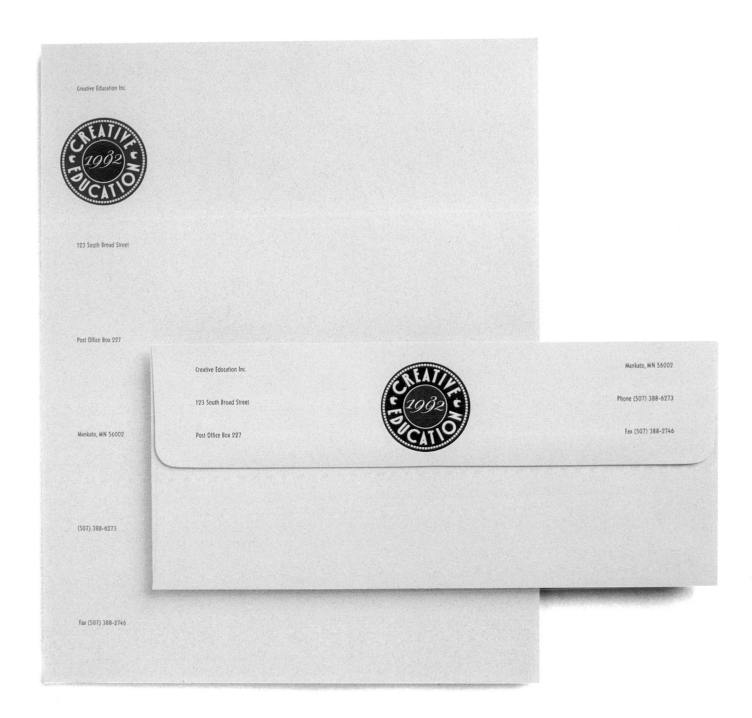

Creative Education Inc.

123 South Broad Street

Post Office Box 227

Mankato, MN 56002

(507) 388-6273

Fax (507) 388-2746

Creative Education Inc.

123 South Broad Street

Post Office Box 227

Mankato, MN 56002

Phone (507) 388-6273

Fax (507) 388-2746

CLIENT: CREATIVE EDUCATION INC.

DESIGN FIRM: DELESSERT-MARSHALL

ART DIRECTOR/DESIGNER: RITA MARSHALL

COUNTRY: USA

CLIENT: SOHO MAGAZINE
DESIGN FIRM: DOUBLING COMMUNICATIONS
ART DIRECTOR/DESIGNER: DAVID ORR
COUNTRY: USA

CLIENT: UPCOUNTRY CANADA INC.
DESIGN FIRM: HAMBLY & WOOLLEY INC.
ART DIRECTORS: BARBARA WOOLLEY, BOB HAMBLY
ILLUSTRATOR: DOUG PANTON
COUNTRY: CANADA

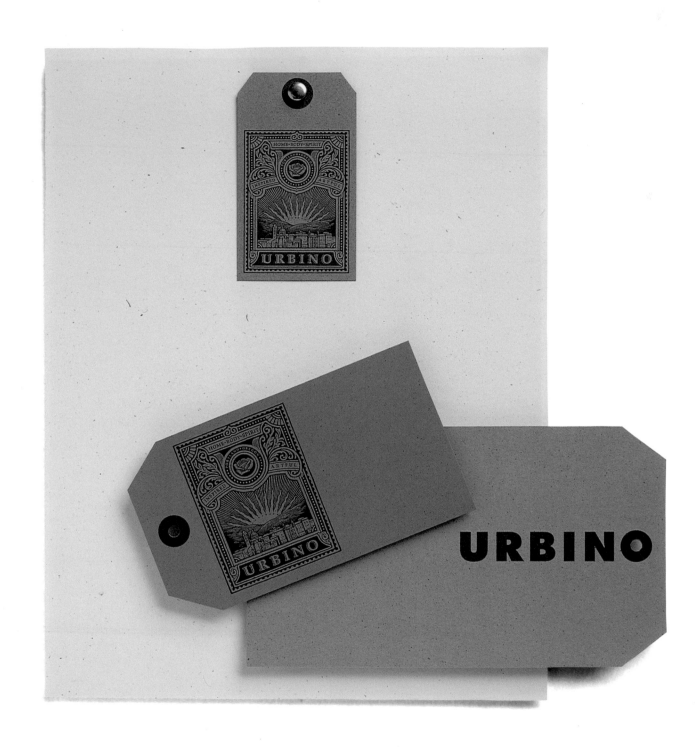

Client: URBINO
Art Directors: ROBIN RICKABAUGH, HEIDI RICKABAUGH
Designers: KIMBERLY LEW, HEIDI RICKABAUGH
Country: USA

MUSEUMS

MUSEEN

MUSÉES

CLIENT: MUSEUM OF CONTEMPORARY ART, SAN DIEGO
DESIGN FIRM: PENTAGRAM DESIGN
ART DIRECTOR: KIT HINRICHS
DESIGNER: SUSAN TSUCHIYA
COUNTRY: USA

CLIENT: MCAD
DESIGN FIRM: C.S. ANDERSON DESIGN CO.
ART DIRECTORS: CHARLES ANDERSON, DANIEL OLSON
DESIGNERS: DANIEL OLSON, CHARLES ANDERSON
COUNTRY: USA

Portland Museum
2308 Portland Avenue
Louisville, Kentucky 40212
(502) 776-7678

Nathalie T. Andrews
Director

Portland Museum
2308 Portland Avenue
Louisville, Kentucky 40212
(502) 776-7678

CLIENT: THE PORTLAND MUSEUM
DESIGN FIRM: IMAGES
ART DIRECTOR: JULIUS FRIEDMAN
DESIGNERS: JULIUS FRIEDMAN, WALTER McCORD
COUNTRY: USA

CLIENT: BM CONTEMPORARY ART CENTER

DESIGN FIRM: REKLAMEVI/YOUNG & RUBICAM

ART DIRECTOR·DESIGNER: BÜLENT ERKMEN

COUNTRY: TURKEY

CLIENT: PORTLAND ART MUSEUM

ART DIRECTORS: ROBIN RICKABAUGH, HEIDI RICKABAUGH

DESIGNERS: KIMBERLY LEW, ROBIN RICKABAUGH

COUNTRY: USA

Galleria Colonna
Largo Chigi, 19
00187 Roma
Tel 06 67721
Fax 06 6772 287

CLIENT: GALLERIA COLONNA
DESIGN FIRM: PENTAGRAM DESIGN
ART DIRECTOR: JOHN McCONNELL
DESIGNER: JUSTUS OEHLER
COUNTRY: ITALY

SCHOOLS

SCHULEN

ECOLES

CLIENT: HIKO MIZUNO COLLEGE OF JEWELRY
DESIGN FIRM: B-BI STUDIO INCORPORATED
ART DIRECTOR/DESIGNER: ZEMPAKU SUZUKI
COUNTRY: JAPAN

CLIENT: NATIONAL COMMUNITY COLLEGE CHAIR ACADEMY
DESIGN FIRM: AFTER HOURS
ART DIRECTOR/DESIGNER: BRAD SMITH
PHOTOGRAPHER: ART HOLEMAN
COUNTRY: USA

CLIENT: BUENA VISTA COLLEGE

DESIGN FIRM: SAYLES GRAPHIC DESIGN

ART DIRECTOR/DESIGNER: JOHN SAYLES

ILLUSTRATOR: JOHN SAYLES

COUNTRY: USA

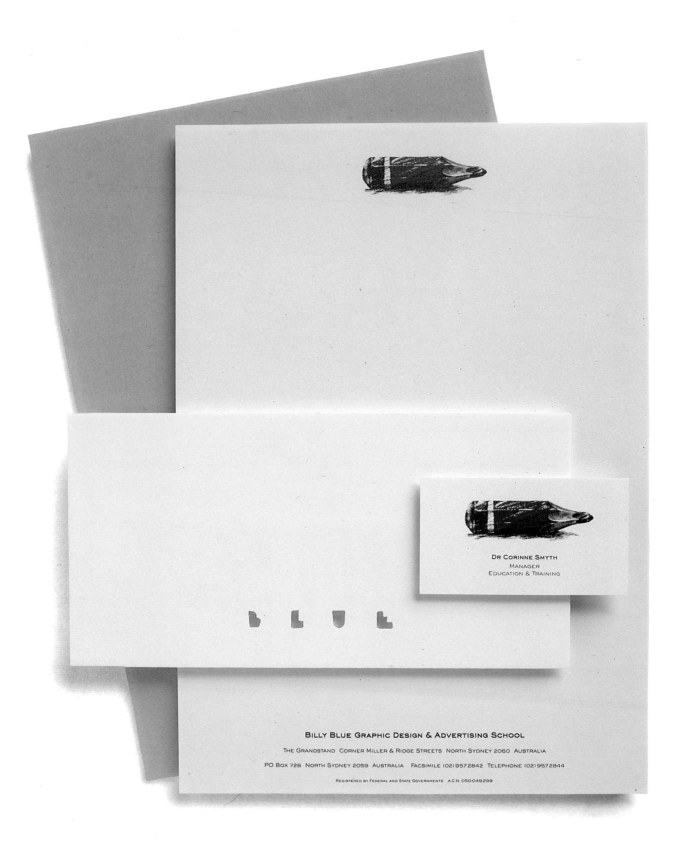

BILLY BLUE GRAPHIC DESIGN & ADVERTISING SCHOOL

THE GRANDSTAND CORNER MILLER & RIDGE STREETS NORTH SYDNEY 2060 AUSTRALIA

PO BOX 728 NORTH SYDNEY 2059 AUSTRALIA FACSIMILE (02) 957 2842 TELEPHONE (02) 957 2844

REGISTERED BY FEDERAL AND STATE GOVERNMENTS A.C.N. 050 049 299

DR CORINNE SMYTH
MANAGER
EDUCATION & TRAINING

CLIENT: BILLY BLUE GROUP
DESIGN FIRM: BILLY BLUE GROUP
ART DIRECTOR/DESIGNER: ROSS RENWICK
COUNTRY: AUSTRALIA

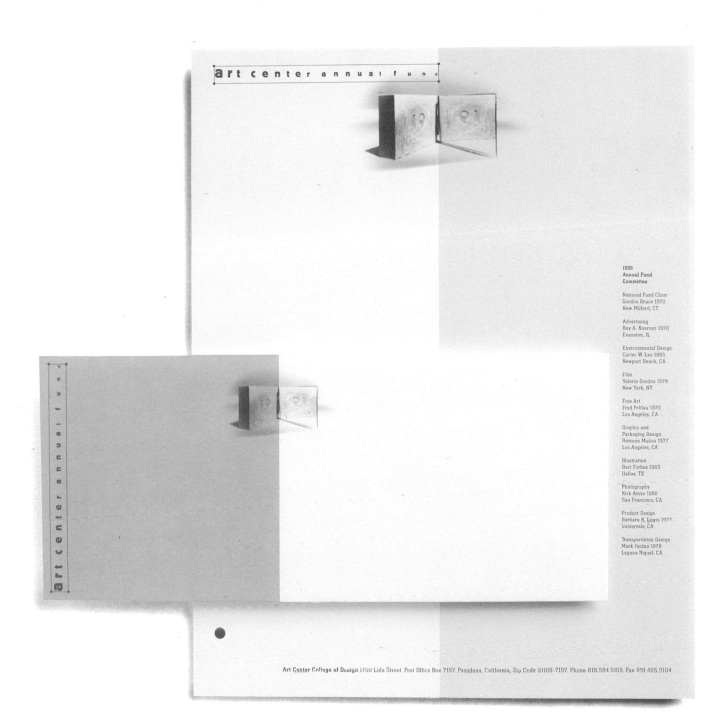

HASHIMOTO

ART INSTITUTE

R. B L D G

4-21-15 HASHIMOTO

SAGAMIHARA-SHI

KANAGAWA

229 JAPAN

TEL 0427-73-4168

FAX 0427-73-8747

FREE 0120-379615

CLIENT: HASHIMOTO ART INSTITUTE
DESIGN FIRM: B-BI STUDIO INCORPORATED
ART DIRECTOR/DESIGNER: ZEMPAKU SUZUKI
COUNTRY: JAPAN

VARIA

VARIA

VARIA

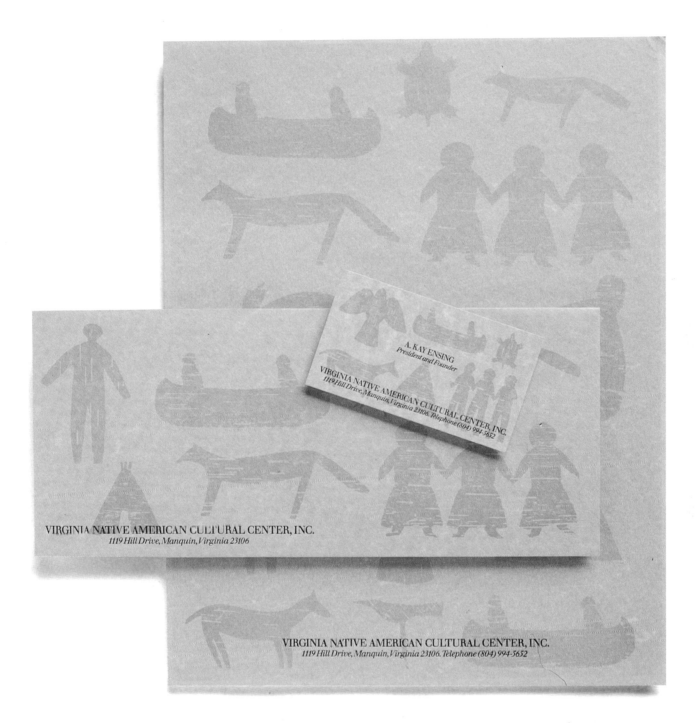

CLIENT: VIRGINIA NATIVE AMERICAN CULTURAL CENTER
DESIGN FIRM: THE MARTIN AGENCY
ART DIRECTOR/DESIGNER: JERRY TORCHIA
COUNTRY: USA

yew bowl by ray key

press release
pers bericht

de beurs in de beurs
the amsterdam international
contemporary crafts fair

	c/o crafts council	crafts council london	dutch form amsterdam
correspondentie:	44a pentonville road	t +44 (0)71 278 7700	t +31 (0)20 638 1120
correspondence:	GB·london n1 9by	f +44 (0)71 837 6891	f +31 (0)20 620 1031

blown glass by robert crooks

de beurs in de beurs
the amsterdam international
contemporary crafts fair

	c/o crafts council	crafts council london	dutch form amsterdam
correspondentie:	44a pentonville road	t +44 (0)71 278 7700	t +31 (0)20 638 1120
correspondence:	GB·london n1 9by	f +44 (0)71 837 6891	f +31 (0)20 620 1031

CLIENT: CRAFTS COUNCIL
ART DIRECTOR: JOHN RUSHWORTH
DESIGNER: NICK FINNEY
COUNTRY: GREAT BRITAIN

CLIENT: EVENTMEDIA INTERNATIONAL INC.
DESIGN FIRM: MICHAEL DORET, INC.
ART DIRECTOR/DESIGNER: MICHAEL DORET
ILLUSTRATOR: MICHAEL DORET
COUNTRY: USA

**THE FARMERS' DAIRY COMPANY
BELONGS TO FARMERS COMMITTED TO
PROVIDING GOOD CHEMICAL-FREE FOOD
AND IMPROVING THE ENVIRONMENT**

THE FARMERS' DAIRY CO LTD
BUSSES FARM, HARWOODS LANE, EAST GRINSTEAD, WEST SUSSEX RH19 4NL, UK
TELEPHONE +44 (0)342 313778 FAX +44 (0)342 313616

VAT REG 602 3889 45 COMPANY REG 269 3802

0 Client: BUSSES FARM, FARMERS DAIRY CO.
Design Firm: PENTAGRAM DESIGN LTD.
Art Director: JOHN RUSHWORTH
Designers: JOHN RUSHWORTH, VINCE FROST
Photographer: STEVE REES
Country: GREAT BRITAIN

JANE GILMOUR

JANE GILMOUR

5/63 DARLING STREET, SOUTH YARRA, VICTORIA 3141
TELEPHONE (03) 820 9280

JANE GILMOUR CONSULTING PTY LTD
5/63 DARLING STREET, SOUTH YARRA, VICTORIA 3141
TELEPHONE (03) 820 9280
ACN 007 045 169

CLIENT: JANE GILMORE CONSULTING PTY LTD
DESIGN FIRM: DAVID LANCASHIRE DESIGN
DESIGNER: DAVID LANCASHIRE
COUNTRY: AUSTRALIA

CLIENT: MARY AND JONATHAN ALEXANDER
DESIGN FIRM: PENTAGRAM
ART DIRECTORS: WOODY PIRTLE, LESLIE PIRTLE
DESIGNER: JENNIFER LONG
COUNTRIES: GREAT BRITAIN, USA

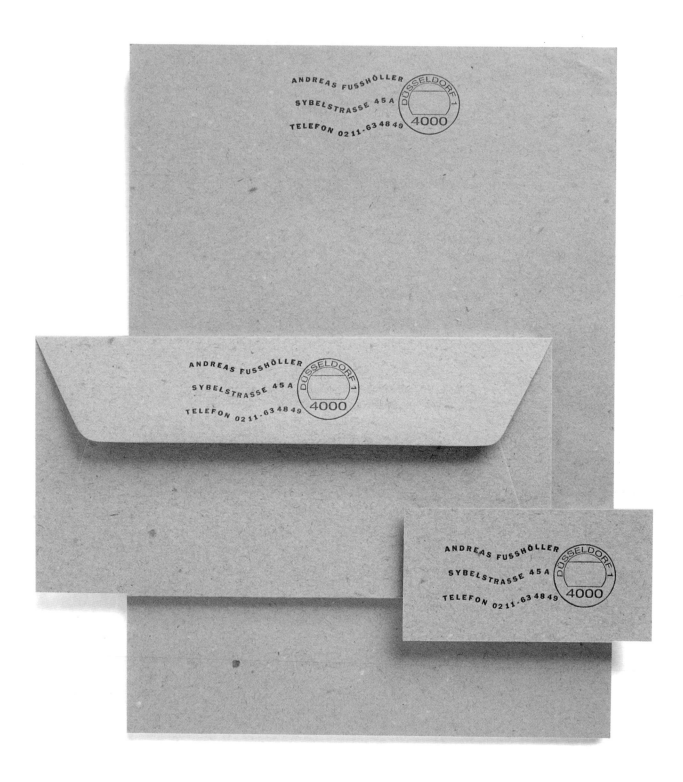

CLIENT: ANDREAS FUSSHÖLLER
ART DIRECTOR: ANDREAS FUSSHÖLLER
COUNTRY: GERMANY

ISABELLA MICHELS, GALVANISTRASSE 24, A-4040 LINZ, TELEFON O 73 2 / 75 94 26

ISABELLA MICHELS, GALVANISTRASSE 24, A-4040 LINZ, TELEFON O 73 2 / 75 94 26

ISABELLA MICHELS, GALVANISTRASSE 24, A-4040 LINZ

ISABELLA MICHELS, GALVANISTRASSE 24, A-4040 LINZ, TELEFON O 73 2 / 75 94 26

CLIENT: ISABELLA MICHELS
DESIGN FIRM: JOSEF PAUSCH
ART DIRECTOR/DESIGNER: JOSEF PAUSCH
COUNTRY: AUSTRIA

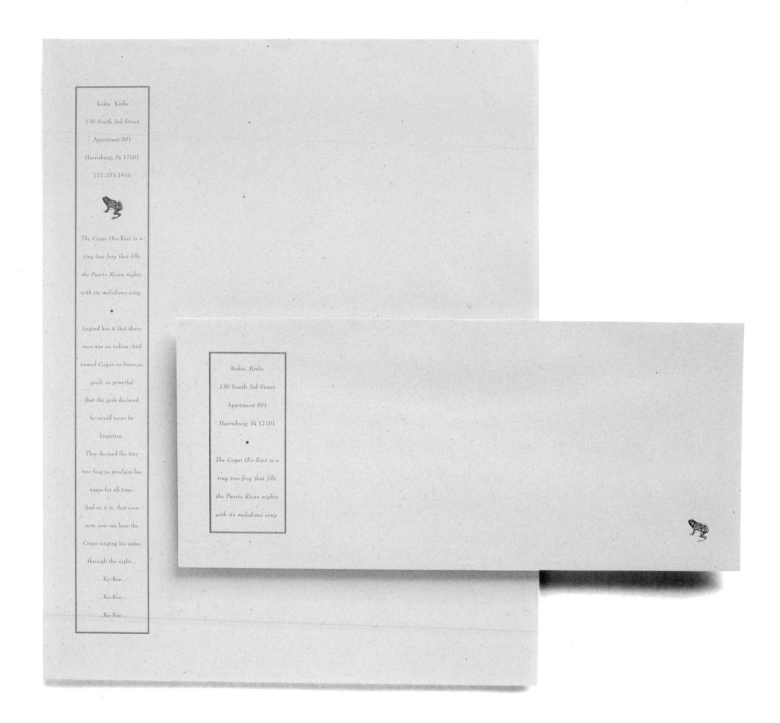

CLIENT: KOKIE KREBS
DESIGN FIRM: WARKULWIZ DESIGN
ART DIRECTOR/DESIGNER: SOONDUK KREBS
COUNTRY: USA

SIX LONGFELLOW ROAD · WELLESLEY HILLS · MASS 02181 · USA

DR. MARK S. ALBION PHD

BUSINESS EDUCATOR

AUTHOR

SIX LONGFELLOW ROAD · WELLESLEY HILLS · MASS 02181 · USA DR. MARK S. ALBION PHD

SIX LONGFELLOW ROAD
WELLESLEY HILLS · MASS 02181
USA
TELEPHONE 617-235-8923
TELEFAX 617-235-1757

DR. MARK S. ALBION PHD · 617-235-8923 · FAX 617-235-1757

CLIENT: DR. MARK S. ALBION
ART DIRECTOR/DESIGNER: KAREN BIRNHOLZ
ILLUSTRATOR: JOHN SCHOUTEN
COUNTRY: USA

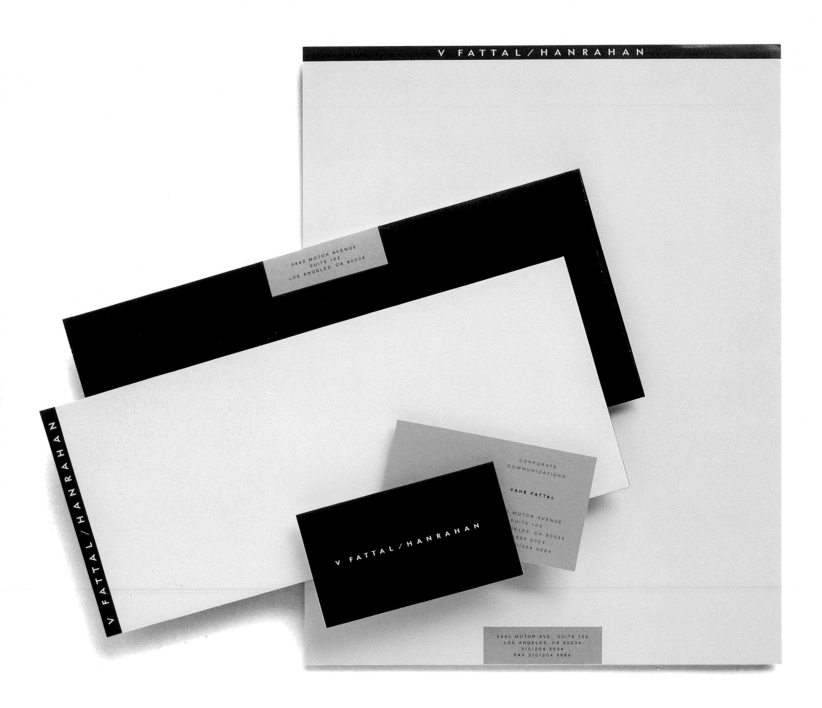

CLIENT: V FATTAL/HANRAHAN
DESIGN FIRM: V FATTAL/HANRAHAN
ART DIRECTOR/DESIGNER: VAHÉ FATTAL
COUNTRY: USA

INDEX

VERZEICHNIS

INDEX

•

CALL FOR ENTRIES

EINLADUNGEN

APPEL D'ENVOIS

Clients

CALL FOR ENTRIES

Graphis Packaging 6 · Entry Deadline: November 30, 1993

■ Food, beverages, tobacco products, cosmetics, fashion, household, industrial products, carrier bags, stationery, promotions, etc. Eligibility: All work produced between December 1989 and November 1993. ● Konsumgüter, Tabakwaren, Kosmetik, Mode, Haushaltartikel sowie Tragtaschen und Einwickelpapier, industrielle Produkte, Promotionsartikel usw. In Frage kommen: Arbeiten, die zwischen Dezember 1989 und November 1993 entstanden sind. ▲ Biens de consommation, tabac, produits cosmétiques, accessoires de mode, articles de ménage, sacs à commissions, papier cadeau, produits industriels, articles de promotion etc. Seront admis: tous travaux réalisés entre décembre 1989 et novembre 1993.

Graphis Poster 95 · Entry Deadline: April 30, 1994

■ Advertising, cultural, and social posters. Eligibility: All work produced between May 1993 and April 1994. ● Plakate für Werbezwecke sowie kulturelle und soziale Plakate. In Frage kommen: Arbeiten, die zwischen Mai 1993 und April 1994 entstanden sind. ▲ Affiches publicitaires, culturelles et sociales. Seront admis: tous les travaux réalisés entre mai 1993 et avril 1994.

Graphis Photo 95 · Entry Deadline: August 31, 1994

■ Ads, catalogs, invitations, announcements, record covers, and calendars on any subject.. Photographs taken for consumer or trade magazines, newspapers, books and corporate publications. Personal studies on any subject. Experimental or student work on any subject. Eligibility: All work produced between September 1993 and August 1994. ● Anzeigen, Kataloge, Plattenhüllen, Kalender. Photos für Zeitschriften, Zeitungen, Bücher und Firmenpublikationen. Persönliche Studien. Experimentelle Aufnahmen oder Studentenarbeiten. In Frage kommen: Arbeiten, die zwischen September 1993 und August 1994 entstanden sind. ▲ Publicité, catalogues, invitations, annonces, pochettes de disques, calendriers. Reportages pour magazines et journaux, livres et publications d'entreprise. Études personnelles, créations expérimentales ou projets d'étudiants. Seront admis: tous les travaux réalisés entre septembre 1993 et août 1994.

Graphis Design 95 · Entry Deadline: November 30, 1993

■ Ads; promotion brochures, catalogs, invitations, record covers, announcements, logos, corporate campaigns, calendars, books, book covers, packaging, company magazines; newspapers, consumer or trade magazines, annual reports; illustration. Eligibility: All work produced between December 1, 1992 and November 30, 1993. ● Werbung, Broschüren, Kataloge, Plattenhüllen, Logos, Firmenkampagnen, Kalender, Bücher, Buchumschläge, Packungen. Zeitschriften, Hauszeitschriften, Jahresberichte, Illustrationen. In Frage kommen: Arbeiten, die zwischen Dezember 1992 und November 1993 entstanden sind. ▲ Publicité; brochures, catalogues, invitations, pochettes de disques, annonces, logos, identité visuelle, calendriers, livres, packaging;journaux, revues, magazines de sociétés, rapports annuels; illustration. Seront admis: les travaux réalisés entre décembre 1992 et novembre 1993.

■ **What to send:** Reproduction-quality duplicate transparencies (4x5" or 35mm). They are required for large, bulky or valuable pieces. ALL 35MM SLIDES MUST BE CARDBOARD-MOUNTED, NO GLASS SLIDE MOUNTS PLEASE! *Please mark the transparencies with your name.* If you do send printed pieces they should be unmounted, but well protected. WE REGRET THAT ENTRIES CANNOT BE RETURNED. ● **Was einsenden:** Wenn immer möglich, schicken Sie uns bitte reproduktionsfähige Duplikatdias. *Bitte Dias mit Ihrem Namen versehen.* Bitte schicken Sie auf keinen Fall Originaldias. KLEINBILDDIAS BITTE IM KARTONRAHMEN, KEIN GLAS! Falls Sie uns das gedruckte Beispiel schicken, bitten wir Sie, dieses gut geschützt aber nicht aufgezogen zu senden. WIR BEDAUERN, DASS EINSENDUNGEN NICHT ZURÜCKGESCHICKT WERDEN KÖNNEN. ■ **Que nous envoyer:** Nous vous recommandons de nous faire parvenir de préférence des duplicata de diapositives (4x5" ou 35mm. N'oubliez pas d'inscrire votre nom dessus). NE PAS ENVOYER DE DIAPOSITIVES SOUS VERRE! Si vous désirez envoyer des travaux imprimés, protégez-les, mais ne les montez pas sur carton. *Nous vous signalons que les envois que vous nous aurez fait parvenir ne pourront vous être retournés.*

■ **How to package your entry:** Please tape (do not glue) the completed entry form (or a copy) to the back of each piece. Please do not send anything by air freight. Write "No Commercial Value" on the package, and label it "Art for Contest." ● **Wie und wohin senden:** Bitte befestigen Sie das ausgefüllte Einsende-etikett (oder eine Kopie davon) mit Klebstreifen (nicht kleben) auf jeder Arbeit und legen Sie noch ein Doppel davon lose bei. Bitte auf keinen Fall Luft- oder Bahnfracht senden. Deklarieren Sie «Ohne jeden Handelswert» und «Arbeitsproben für Wettbewerb». ▲ **Comment préparer votre envoi:** Veuillez scotcher (ne pas coller) au dos de chaque spécimen les étiquettes dûment remplies. Nous vous prions également de faire un double de chaque étiquette, que vous joindrez à votre envoi, mais sans le coller ou le fixer. Ne nous expédiez rien en fret aérien. Indiquez «Sans aucune valeur commerciale» et «Echantillons pour concours».

■ **Entry fees** Single entries: United States U.S. $15; Germany, DM 15,00; all other countries, SFr 15.00. Three or more pieces entered in a single contest: North America, U.S. $35, Germany DM 40,00, All other countries SFr 40.00. These entry fees do not apply to countries with exchange controls or to students (please send copy of student identification). ● **Einsendegebühren:** Für jede einzelne Arbeit: Deutschland DM 15.00, alle andern Länder SFr 15.00. Für jede Kampagne oder Serie von drei oder mehr Stück: Deutschland DM 40.00, übrige Länder SFr 40.00. Für Studenten (Ausweiskopie mitschicken) und Länder mit Devisenbeschränkugen gelten diese Einsendegebühren nicht. ▲ **Droits d'admission**: Envoi d'un seul travail: pour l'Amérique du Nord, US$ 15.00; pour tous les autres pays: SFr. 15.00. Campagne ou série de trois travaux ou plus pour un seul concours: Amérique du Nord, US$ 35.00; autres pays: SFr. 40.00. Les participants de pays qui connaissent des restrictions monétaires sont dispensés des droits d'admission, au même titre que les étudiants (veuillez envoyer une photocopie de la carte d'étudiant).

■ **Where to send:** Entries from the United States and Canada should be sent to the New York office and checks should be made payable to GRAPHIS US, INC, NEW YORK. Entries from all other countries should be sent to the Zurich office and checks should be made payable to GRAPHIS PRESS CORP., ZURICH. ● **Wohin senden:** Bitte senden Sie uns Ihre Arbeiten an Graphis Zürich zusammen mit einem Scheck, ausgestellt in SFr. (auf eine Schweizer Bank ziehen oder Eurocheck) oder überweisen Sie den Betrag auf PC Luzern 60-3520-6 oder PSchK Frankfurt 3000 57-602 (BLZ 50010060). ▲ **Où envoyer:** Veuillez envoyer vos travaux à Graphis Zurich et joindre un chèque tiré sur une banque suisse ou un Eurochèque; ou verser le montant sur le compte chèque postal Lucerne 60–3520-6.

Graphis Press, Dufourstrasse 107, CH-8008 Zürich, Switzerland, telephone: 41-1-383 82 11, fax: 41-1-383 16 43
Graphis US, Inc., 141 Lexington Avenue, New York, NY 10016, telephone: (212) 532 9387, fax: (212) 213 3229

E N T R Y   F O R M

I wish to enter the attached in the following Graphis competition:

. . . .

☐ **GRAPHIS PACKAGING 6**

(NOVEMBER 30, 1993)

CATEGORY

CODES/KATEGORIEN/CATÉGORIES

PA1 FOOD/NAHRUNGSMITTEL/
ALIMENTATION

PA2 BEVERAGES/GETRÄNKE/
BOISSONS

PA3 TOBACCO/TABAK-
WAREN/TABAC

PA4 COSMETICS/KOSMETIK/
COSMÉTIQUES

PA5 FASHION/MODE

PA6 HOUSEHOLD/HAUSHALT/
MÉNAGE

PA7 CARRIER BAGS/TRAG-
TASCHEN/SACS

PA8 INDUSTRY/INDUSTRIE

PA9 PROMOTION

PA10 MISCELLANEOUS/
ANDERE/AUTRES

☐ **GRAPHIS POSTER 95**

(APRIL 30, 1994)

CATEGORY

CODES/KATEGORIEN/CATÉGORIES

PO1 ADVERTISING/WERBUNG/
PUBLICITÉ

PO2 CULTURE/KULTUR

PO3 SOCIAL/GESELLSCHAFT/
SOCIÉTÉ

☐ **GRAPHIS PHOTO 95**

(AUGUST 31, 1994)

CATEGORY

CODES/KATEGORIEN/CATÉGORIES

PH1 FASHION/MODE

PH2 JOURNALISM/
JOURNALISMUS

PH3 STILL LIFE/STILLEBEN/
NATURE MORTE

PH4 FOOD/LEBENSMITTEL/
CUISINE

PH5 PEOPLE/MENSCHEN/
PERSONNES

PH6 PRODUCTS/PRODUKTE/
PRODUITS

PH7 OUTDOORS/LAND-
SCHAFT/EXTÉRIEURS

PH8 ARCHITECTURE/
ARCHITEKTUR/

PH9 WILD LIFE/TIERE/
ANIMAUX

PH10 SPORTS/SPORT

PH11 FINE ART/KUNST/ART

☐ **GRAPHIS DESIGN 95**

(NOVEMBER 30, 1993)

CATEGORY

CODES/KATEGORIEN/CATÉGORIES

DE1 ADVERTISING/WERBUNG/
PUBLICITÉ

DE2 BOOKS/BÜCHER/
LIVRES

DE3 BROCHURES/BROSCHÜREN

DE4 EDITORIAL/REDAKTIONELL/
RÉDACTIONNEL

DE5 PHOTOGRAPHY/
PHOTOGRAPHIE

DE6 ILLUSTRATION

DE7 CORPORATE IDENTITY

DE8 PACKAGING/VER-
PACKUNG

DE9 CALENDARS/KALENDER/
CALENDRIERS

DE10 MISCELLANEOUS/
ANDERE/DIVERS

TAPE (DON'T GLUE) A COMPLETED COPY OF THIS FORM TO THE BACK OF EACH ENTRY

BITTE AUF DER RÜCKSEITE JEDER ARBEIT MIT KLEBBAND BEFESTIGEN
VEUILLEZ SCOTCHER (NE PAS COLLER) AU DOS DE CHAQUE ENVOI

TITLE OF ENTRY _____

CATEGORY CODE   YEAR CREATED/PUBLISHED

PERSON/COMPANY ENTERING WORK

PRINT NAME _____

TITLE _____

COMPANY _____

ADDRESS _____

CITY   STATE

COUNTRY _____

TELEPHONE   FAX

I hereby grant permission for the attached material to be published in
any Graphis book, article in *Graphis* magazine, or any advertisement,
brochure or other material produced for the purpose of promoting
Graphis publications.

SIGNATURE   DATE

TITEL DER ARBEIT
TITRE DE L'ENVOI

KATEGORIENCODE   ENTSTANDEN/PUBLIZIERT
CODE DE CATÉGORIE   CRÉÉ/PUBLIÉ (ANNÉE)

NAME DES EINSENDERS
TRAVAIL ENVOYÉ PAR

TITEL/TITRE

FIRMA/SOCIÉTÉ

ADRESSE

PLZ/STADT/LAND
VILLE/CODE POSTAL/PAYS

TELEPHON   FAX

Ich erteile Graphis hiermit das Recht zur Veröffentlichung meiner Arbeit in
den Graphis-Büchern oder in der Zeitschrift *Graphis* sowie in Anzeigen
oder Broschüren zu Werbezwecken der Graphis-Publikationen.
Par la présente, j'autorise les Editions Graphis à publier le travail ci-joint
dans tout livre Graphis, dans tout article du magazine *Graphis*, ainsi que
tout matériel publicitaire, brochure, dépliant ou autre, destiné à la promotion des publication Graphis.

DATUM   UNTERSCHRIFT
DATE   SIGNATURE

Mail entries to:
Graphis Press, Dufourstrasse 107, CH-8008 Zürich, or
Graphis US, Inc., 141 Lexington Ave, New York, NY 10016

Bitte senden Sie Ihre Arbeit an/Veuillez envoyer à l'adresse suivante::
Graphis Verlag AG, Dufourstrasse 107, CH-8008 Zürich,
Schweiz, Telephon: 01-383-82-11, Telefax: 01-383-16-43

GRAPHIS PHOTO

GRAPHIS LETTERHEAD

GRAPHIS POSTER

88 89 90 91 92 93

GRAPHIS ANNUAL REPORTS

1 2 3

N U D E S

GRAPHIS DESIGN

89 90 91 92 93

▶ AVAILABLE IN EARLY 1994

▶ AVAILABLE IN EARLY 1994

▶ AVAILABLE IN MID 1994

GRAPHIS TYPOGRAPHY

A B C D E
F G H I J
K L M N O
P Q R S T
U V W X Y
Z ! ? &

RECYCLED PAPERS

COATED PAPERS

UNCOATED PAPERS

3 2 1

G R A P H I S   B O O K S